So Clear, So Cool, So Grand

. . . it was a glorious day; so clear, so cool, so grand.
There was nothing which could possibly destroy
the perfect harmony between us and nature.

So Clear, So Cool, So Grand

A 1931 HIKE
ON
VERMONT'S LONG TRAIL

By

JAMES GORDON HINDES

Edited by Reidun D. Nuquist

With a Foreword by Robert P. Northrop

The Green Mountain Club
Waterbury Center, Vermont

The Green Mountain Club, Inc.
4711 Waterbury Stowe Road
Waterbury Center, Vermont 05677
802-244-7037
www.greenmountainclub.org

Ben Rose, Executive Director
Arthur Goldsweig, Director of Finance
Susan Shea, Director of Conservation and Managing Editor

GMC Publications Committee, 2008:
Richard Andrews, Dave Blumenthal, Ruth Hare,
Lynda Hutchins, Steve Larose, Mary Lou Recor, Val Stori

Book design by Sylvie Vidrine

FRONT COVER:
Camel's Hump.
Courtesy of Vermont Historical Society.
James Gordon Hindes on Killington Peak.
Courtesy of Hindes family.

BACK COVER:
Hindes and John P. Eames on the Long Trail.
Courtesy of Hindes family.

ISBN 978-188802123-3-50895

Printed with soy-based inks.

Contents

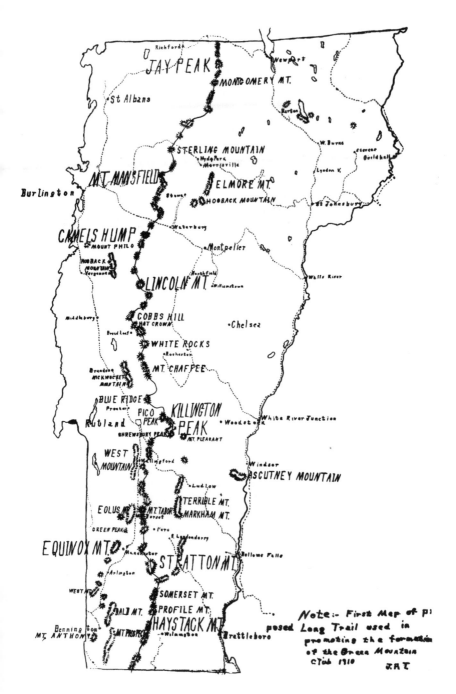

James P. Taylor's sketch map of the Long Trail, 1910.
GMC.

Foreword

The account by James Gordon Hindes of his 1931 end-to-end hike on the fledgling Long Trail brings back many memories of my own 1937 and 1938 treks. It has always been a disappointment to me that I neglected to chronicle my two first hikes, better to remember and re-live my ups and downs, both figuratively and literally. Too many details of those days are lost memories. Therefore, I deeply appreciate the thorough and entertaining account of *his* hike.

My earliest Long Trail hikes—I was sixteen the first time—were seminal events of my teenage years, events which influenced my growing up almost more than anything else, except perhaps for the initial inspiration to climb mountains, which came from my father, Albert Allen Northrop. He introduced me to the Berkshires, to the White Mountains, and encouraged me every step of the way. From my father I learned to love the freedom and aloneness of hiking.

There was one other event in my father's life that inspired me and that was the fact that he participated in the Gold Rush of 1898 in the Klondike. He hiked up the sometimes deadly Chilkoot Pass and Trail, found gold, came back richer, and invested his money in a bank, which promptly failed. However, this financial setback did not dampen his love for mountain climbing. And I was the richer for that.

When Hindes and I enjoyed the Long Trail in the 1930s, Vermont was a more open and agrarian place than the heavily forested state of today. Hindes encountered many upland farms, as did I. I observed wood-cutting crews from the Civilian Conservation Corps (CCC), which provided much needed work and new skills for an economically depressed nation. We both encountered many more porcupines and other wild critters than we see these days. Then, as well as now, there were some bear; moose seem to be a recent addition to Vermont's trails.

In the thirties, and even later, camp fires were tolerated and perhaps encouraged. I built one or two cooking fires each day, as did Hindes; for the last thirty years or so cooking has been mostly by small, efficient camp stoves. Today, the protection of flora and fauna is of paramount importance to all of us.

It is a distinct privilege to have hiked Vermont's Long Trail end to end seven times. My last hike was in 2001 with my son Stephen and grandson Robert. It was just as grand then as Hindes described it in 1931. The energy expanded is rewarded many-fold by the silent but awesome beauty of our Green Mountains.

Finally, I appreciate the reference by James Gordon Hindes to that wonderful mountain, Le Lion Couchant (also known as Camel's Hump). It has always looked like a couching lion to me. But whether camel or lion, it remains one of the most wonderful sights of the Vermont landscape and is always a thrill to climb.

Robert P. Northrop

A Tribute to James Gordon Hindes (1909–1973) by his Children

Din grasps the starboard gunwale of the wooden skiff with his left hand, places his right under the prow so his elbow points up and behind his strong narrow shoulder. He twists his canvas shoes into the smooth, bean-shaped stones that cover the beach to get enough purchase to push the small skiff free and into the still water of Lake Champlain. He steadies the bow as she settles herself in. Overhead some gulls screek to one another. Din squints into the late day sun to watch them circle and land in the bay. He stuffs his duffle full of camping gear under the skiff's front seat. Then, with one movement, he throws a leg over the gunwale and lands on the seat between the oarlocks. The pins fastened on the dark green oars fit firmly into the locks. The youth leans back pulling the oars to his chest, takes a glance at the New York shore a mile across the lake to sight in Barn Rock Harbor. With one grand sweep of his arm, he waves to his father and mother who wave back.

They lean forward in their rocking chairs, peering through the screens on the wide front porch of their cottage, the Elmwood, as their teenage son rows along a familiar course toward his favorite campsite. It is near twilight when the boat slides out of sight into a cove near Barn Rock Harbor. They watch the opposite shore waiting for the agreed upon signal of his safe arrival. They are soon assured by the flash of a white flag being nudged by a bit of southerly air atop Din's driftwood flagpole that he and his father erected at the beginning of summer. When night comes, the glow of his campfire spreads toward them on the surface of the lake. All but one light goes out in the Elmwood.

The damp coolness of night air flows down, over, and through the trees behind where Din is bedded down. He pulls the wool blanket closer. Whirring pines, a whippoorwill, and the high, thin hum of insects above the soft comfort of Lake Champlain's waters make a kind of nightsong that will last until dawn again rises up from the Green Mountains.

———

James Gordon Hindes was born in Winchester, Massachusetts, in 1909. He was a multi-generation Vermonter (great-great grandson of John Hindes, an early settler of Addison), a proud son of Lake

James Gordon Hindes at Mile Point, Lake Champlain, ca. 1931.
Courtesy of Hindes family.

Champlain and the Green Mountains. Though he was named James Gordon, his parents decided he would be called by his middle name. His young mother, however, perhaps feeling Gordon was too weighty a name for her tiny baby began calling him Din, and so family and schoolmates would call him Din from then on.

As a young outdoorsman, Din spent every summer of his youth in Vermont, at family cottages on Mile Point in Ferrisburgh or at Camp Sangamon in Pittsford. He graduated from Vermont Academy in 1928 and from Dartmouth College in 1932. His 1931 diary records one of the earliest "end-to-end" hikes on the Long Trail, made the summer between his junior and senior years of college.

By the time he graduated from college, the country had slipped into the Great Depression. Din's search for work carried him from the classrooms of New England to meat packing plants in the Midwest, to roughnecking in Texas oil fields, and finally into the US Army. During his years as a student, he had developed his aptitude for writing as well as an affinity for French language and culture—all of which he would utilize during an extended tour in the European theater in the Second World War and through his long military career in what would become the US Air Force.

He retired from the military in 1962, moved our family to Vermont, and began a second career as a high school English teacher in Highgate. A dream fulfilled at last.

Our grandmother, Patience Chase Hindes, was an accomplished classical pianist. Our Vermont-born grandfather, J. Churchill Hindes, was a dentist who lent his fine bass voice to choral groups throughout much of his life. Music and an unquenchable love of nature, and all things Vermont, became inseparable parts of our father's being from the time he was a young child.

As a father this was manifested, to our delight, by the way he introduced us children to classical music. One evening he might select a Brahms symphony and gather us on the floor near the big Zenith, an imposing piece of furniture that housed a radio and record player. We'd sit cross-legged on the floor, listen for the clack made by the 78-record when it dropped onto the turntable, and wait for the music to begin. What followed was a wondrous journey into a world of forests, lakes, and granite cliffs, inhabited by fish, birds, waddling porcupines, cavorting otters, and bears eating blueberries. With every musical movement, father's vivid imagination delivered brilliant narratives accompanied by elaborate gestures, some of which required dancing around the room.

Each change in the music brought a different scene. There was quiet listening time to identify various instruments in the orchestra. The evening's tale nearly always included an orchestral thunderstorm that rolled and echoed through the Green Mountains and down to Mile Point on Lake Champlain where the family in the Elmwood would sit safe and snug by the fire, listening to the thrum of rain on the roof—a signal for us to head up to our beds.

No matter where our father's career in the Air Force took us, he always found places for his family to be outdoors: the big park in Boston, a kite-flying meadow in Zenia, Ohio, historic places in Washington, D.C., and, in Germany, the many cycling and walking trails through deep green forests that led to villages we enjoyed.

James Gordon Hindes died in December 1973, leaving his Texas-born wife Vesta, and their four children Sybil, Churchill, Teresa, and Christopher. He so cherished his family that he, with our mother, created a family culture and living legacy of unity, love, spirituality, the importance of silliness, appreciation of the arts, and our Vermont and Texas heritages.

Our father always found joy in Vermont's diverse gifts. The happy times of discovery and adventure on the Long Trail in 1931 inhabited a special place in his heart. He was undeniably a man "of" Vermont, and when away from her, longed to be in the nurture of the unyielding beauty of her Green Mountains and all that surrounds them.

For us, Din's children, Vermont—its geography, beauty, character, and memories—is also a most revered place.

Sybil Hindes Hearn
J. Churchill Hindes
Teresa Hindes Didehbani
Christopher Gordon Hindes

Introduction

As a Green Mountain Club historian, I have over the years read hundreds of Long Trail end-to-end accounts. Among these, that of James Gordon Hindes has always stood out as deserving of a wider audience. Not just because his is one of the earliest such reports or because he tells us what it was like hiking long distance in Vermont during the first half of the twentieth century, but also because his account is lively, interesting, and well written. Adding to our reading pleasure, the author comes across as a likeable, enthusiastic, and competent young man with his life still ahead of him.

Hindes hiked the Long Trail (LT) with a Dartmouth College fraternity brother, John (Jack) P. Eames, in the summer of 1931. Only the year before, the trail had finally reached Canada. It had taken Green Mountain Club (GMC) pioneers two decades to cut the then 250-mile-long[1] trail atop the Green Mountains, from the Massachusetts line to the Canadian border. The LT was the first long-distance hiking trail in the United States and became the inspiration for the Appalachian Trail.

In some respects the experience of Hindes was similar to that of today's hiker. He complained when his pack was too heavy, he cussed at no-see-ums and stinging nettles, he grumbled when he lost the trail. He frequently got soaked to the skin—finding the touted Footpath in the Wilderness more an interminable Footbath in the Wilderness. (The summer of 1931 was both wetter and warmer than normal for New England.)

In other ways, his 1931 end-to-end hike was markedly different. Gear and equipment, although up to date for the time, were heavy and cumbersome. His copy of the *Guide Book of the Long Trail* (8th ed., 1930) recommended that the hiker wear hobnailed Munson-last army shoes with wool stockings, canvas or leather leggings (known as puttees), woolen underwear, flannel shirt, and "a light waterproof coat or fishing shirt"—Hindes took a poncho.

In his knapsack or pack basket the well-equipped hiker carried ground cloth, wool blanket, wool sweater, extra woolen socks, flannel pajamas, towel, medicine kit, matches in waterproof container, electric flash lamp or candle lantern, camp axe, whetstone, folding water bucket, can opener, cooking utensils, tin cup and plate, silverware, canteen, and food.

Provisions might include bread wrapped in waxed paper, flour, rice, macaroni, dried beef, bacon, canned goods—such as sauerkraut, baked beans, soups, and peaches—tea, coffee, and cocoa. After reprovisioning along the way, Hindes sometimes carried sixty pounds on his back.

In 1931, Long Trail camps and lodges were new or just a few years old. Many were enclosed structures furnished with wooden bunks, table, a wood stove, and miscellaneous pots and pans. Etiquette required the hiker to replace the firewood he used during his stay. Where there were gaps in overnight accommodations, the *Guide Book* recommended local farms or tourist homes, earning owners some extra cash during the Great Depression that followed the 1929 Wall Street stock market crash. Farms were also sources of fresh provisions, such as eggs, milk, butter, bread, and, if you were really fortunate, apple pie.

Calling home could be a challenge in the early days of the LT. If you were lucky enough to locate a telephone, you turned a hand crank to alert central—which might stay open just a few hours a day. Hindes, understandably, became exasperated when trying to arrange for his father to pick him up at the end of the hike. Forty-two families shared one telephone line: "no wonder news travels fast around Montgomery Center!!"

Perhaps the greatest difference between the LT experience of Hindes and that of today's hiker was the persistent presence of porcupines, called porkies or hedgehogs. Long Trail lodges and camps were under constant attack by porcupines, who chewed—loudly and mostly at night—on any wood that held salt, sodium being absent from their leafy diet. The 1930 *Guide Book of the Long Trail* advised hikers to carry an axe or hatchet and kill porkies on sight, afterward removing their bodies "so they do not create a nuisance." One hiker reported killing twenty on one trip and fifty-four in all. (Vermont's porcupine population diminished sharply after 1959 with the reintroduction of the fisher, a natural porcupine predator.)

The journal of James Gordon Hindes is imbued with a young man's affection for Vermonters and Vermont. On one farm, he finds "real honest-to-goodness folk, attractive by virtue of their simplicity and frankness. Not the slightest sign of artificiality could be detected in their character." The Long Trail landscape often evokes inspired writing: "The brook was full. The water rushed over the brink, swooped downward, flew into shimmering pieces when it struck the rocks below." Choosing the right words was clearly important to the future English teacher.

Hindes and Eames took the time to *enjoy* their through-hike. Hindes thought that those "who rush along attempting to set records, those who are a bit afraid to come into camp an hour later than they had planned, lose the very heart of the trail." He and Eames listened to bird song, admired the scenery, visited with people they met along the way. At Griffith Lake, local fishermen shared "a mess of twenty-five trout for lunch. . . . It wasn't very long before we had eaten them and crawled into bed for a much needed rest."

Every so often the duo left the trail, hitchhiking to the nearest town for a haircut, a movie, or dinner and a pint. In Pittsford, Hindes visited Camp Sangamon, the boys' camp where he had spent summers. On Mount Mansfield, his and Eames' parents arrived by automobile to spend some time with the young men. Occasionally, Hindes and Eames were forced to take an extra day somewhere, to allow the latter, younger by two years and a less seasoned hiker, to nurse his blisters and delicate digestive system.

Hindes and Eames hiked the LT south to north—and had to read the 1930 *Guide Book*, arranged north to south, backward. They were on the trail for more than a month, from July 4 to August 11. On seven of those days they did not hike. When they did, they averaged 9 miles a day. On their longest day, they covered the 17 miles from Boyce Lodge to Battell Lodge; on their shortest they walked the 2.3 miles from the Mount Mansfield Hotel to Barnes Camp in Smugglers' Notch.

What inspired Hindes to tackle the Long Trail in 1931? The recently finished trail was much in the news at the time. The *Vermonter* magazine and the *Long Trail News* carried numerous articles, some of them enthusiastic firsthand accounts by hikers. Traversing the trail was—and still is—an appealing challenge for a fit young person like Hindes. The hike allowed him to forget studies and grades, family and social obligations, and perhaps worries about finding suitable employment upon graduation.

Although from Winchester, Massachusetts, and attending college in Hanover, New Hampshire, Hindes had strong family ties to Vermont. He had spent summers on Lake Champlain and at Camp Sangamon in Pittsford, where boys learned practical skills and "rudimentary agriculture," and went on hikes; Sangamon's progressive founder, Leone E. Smith, was a member of the Green Mountain Club. A contemporary camp brochure tells how campers could reach the Long Trail at Noyes Pond in two hours, and "the highest honor we yet have is a beautiful trip to Mount Mansfield, the highest in Vermont."

At Vermont Academy, the preparatory school Hindes attended in Saxtons River, the curriculum had emphasized "life in the open." This was the school where James P. Taylor, founder of the Green Mountain Club, had been assistant principal, where he had started an outing club, and where the lack of trails in the Green Mountains had moved him to first envision the Long Trail. Although Taylor was long gone by the time Hindes arrived, Taylor's legacy lived on at the school.

Dartmouth College also had strong outdoor traditions. Hindes was a member of the Dartmouth Outing Club, the oldest such club in the Northeast, founded in 1909 by Fred Harris of Brattleboro, Vermont. Other colleges followed suit in the 1920s and 1930s, but it was only at Dartmouth, according to historians Laura and Guy Waterman, that "all students were automatically assumed to be members."

Readers of the journal of James Gordon Hindes may wonder what happened to his hiking companion, Jack Eames of Northboro, Massachusetts. After leaving Dartmouth, he earned a graduate degree from the Massachusetts Institute of Technology, went to work for Standard Oil Development Company, moved to Elizabeth, New Jersey, and died young. Hindes, as described by his children, followed a different career path, one that eventually led him back to Vermont.

And what about Dottie, you may ask, the young woman to whom he dedicated his Long Trail journal? She and Hindes were college sweethearts. Though they were close then, the relationship apparently faded after they set out to pursue individual interests.

———

Hindes called his 1931 journal, typed up the following year, *Notes on the Long Trail of Vermont.* It is presented here as he wrote it, with his spelling and punctuation intact. Where today's reader may need clarification, I have supplied assistance in brackets or notes. The original manuscript is in the possession of the Hindes family. A photocopy is available for study at the Vermont Historical Society Library in Barre.

I am deeply grateful to the Hindes family for allowing the Green Mountain Club to publish the Long Trail journal. The family's support and enthusiasm for the project have been exemplary. I also thank the GMC Publications Committee, particularly Chair Steve Larose and Mary Lou Recor, for their cooperation; Development and Communications Assistant Matt Larson for help with the illustrations; and my friend Kathryn Gohl for professional editorial advice.

The publication of *So Clear, So Cool, So Grand* anticipates the 2010 centennial of the Green Mountain Club and the Long Trail. More than 3,500 hikers have walked the trail from end to end since 1943, when the GMC began keeping count. For them, the journal of James Gordon Hindes is a bridge to the past, a past that is at the same time familiar and unknown.

Reidun D. Nuquist
Montpelier, Vermont.
October 2008

NOTES ON
THE LONG TRAIL OF
VERMONT

Pico Peak and Long Trail Lodge from Deer Leap Mountain.
Courtesy of Vermont Historical Society.

To my fiancée, who was a constant companion and inspiration while I was on the Long Trail, I lovingly dedicate this diary.

———•———

This is an account of a trip I took during the summer of nineteen hundred and thirty-one with my fraternity brother John Eames.

To lovers of nature, I trust that it will be more than a mere record. I hope that they will find in it something which will bring an added insight to their present love of the out-of-doors.

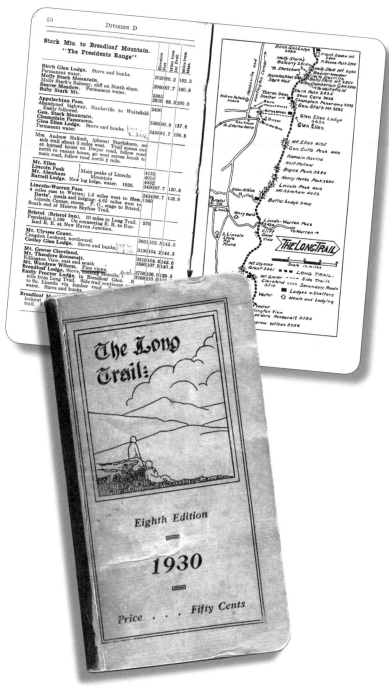

"Guide Book of the Long Trail" (1930).
GMC.

FOREWORD

THE simplicity and earnestness of a life in the out-of-doors presents a great contrast to the confusion and artificiality of life in the city. In the latter, a person does little more than merely exist, while in the case of the former, he becomes aware of some precious seeing—he enjoys a fullness which is consummate.

HARDSHIPS which are inevitable make little joys seem infinitely greater than they otherwise would appear. Living in the woods is not an easy life, it calls upon man's determination until this trait becomes virtually exhausted. A lover of nature never gives up, in fact, he often revels in pitting his strength against forces which beset him. The highest satisfaction which he knows, is to triumph. The struggle and its compensations form an endless chain of grand adventures and glorious reflections upon them.

THE realization of absolute loveliness is the reward which I treasure more dearly than any other. To tender its preciousness has done more to make days seem a little brighter, ideals a little closer, than any material reward which has ever come to me. Ever since childhood, I have been taught that personal satisfaction and delight are worth more than all the riches in the world. The truth of that teaching is more evident to me now than it has ever been. Any man who has ever experienced such a revelation with nature as THE LONG TRAIL affords, knows this.

IF any man wishes to sincerely find himself, let him strap a pack on his back, turn to glories of nature, and drink deeply. Surely, there can be no other test which will prove his worth—or weakness—more conclusively. Toil until the loftiest peaks are conquered, stand upon them and feel a careless wind sweep across your face, survey the vastness at your feet, and when eventide falls, make a bough-bed and let the stars watch over you!

Hanover, New Hampshire
May 22, 1932

Hindes and Eames.
Courtesy of Hindes family.

INTRODUCTION

Although I am not a Vermonter by birth, the many months which I have spent in the state have won my deepest affection for it. Ever since I can remember, my happiest moments have been spent in it, or have been a direct result of the ideals which I have formed from being there.

I have always had the desire to know its broad valleys, its Green Mountains, its sequestered woods, in short, all the gloriousness which nature has bestowed upon it, more fully. Its rural folk are close to my heart, it has been a constant regret of mine that I do not know them better. For, each time I have the opportunity to associate with them, I learn to love them more deeply. They are a noble race in their frank simplicity and they come as near knowing the fullness of true life as is possible in this day.

During my stays in Vermont, I have taken many trips into the mountains, have hiked over sections of the LONG TRAIL. Last March, I made up my mind that the following summer would find me travelling the entire length of the trail.

One evening, while talking with John Eames, I asked him if he would like to accompany me on the trip. As he glanced over the literature of the Green Mountain Club, he became more and more enthusiastic. A letter was sent to his folks asking their permission to go . . . . Easter vacation passed . . . . On our return to college we began to make definite plans for the hike and by the time that the semester's work was completed, arrangements were quite well in hand. The tentative date for departure was set for July 1st.

———

During the last week of June, Jack visited me at my home in Winchester, Massachusetts, and we made final arrangements for our adventure. There was hiking equipment to be bought, letters sent to farmers, whose homes were near the trail, so that our mail might be sent to them and board and lodging procured. An intensive study of trail charts had to be made that we might know how to apportion our food supplies to the intervals at which the trail approaches towns.

The first day of July I dressed myself in hiking clothes, put away my "civilian attire" until my return, and left home. Towards the middle of the afternoon, I reached Jack's home in Northboro, Massachusetts, where I stayed with him until the morning of the third. Our days were busy enough, being spent, for the most part, in checking over details which, on such an undertaking as we were about to enter upon, are absolutely essential.

The afternoon of the second, we took our first important step—the first installment of food was purchased and divided between us, then packed. The eve of departure had arrived. The next day would see us in North Adams, Massachusetts, within a few miles of the southern end of "The Path in the Wilderness."

Vermont–Massachusetts state line.
Courtesy of University of Vermont. Bailey/Howe Library.

JULY 3RD.

In the morning John, his folks, and I left Northboro for Fitchburg, Massachusetts, where we caught the "Minute Man," crack Boston and Maine train, for North Adams. It was a beautiful summer's day and our trip over was uneventful, save for setting the rear brake bands of the automobile a-smouldering. This delayed us for a few minutes outside of Leominster but not enough to hurry us to the station.

At the call for supper, my companion and I eased ourselves into the dining-car, clad in hiking clothes. Our odd appearance caused a little more than ordinary notice from the others present, but as our shoes were still naked—having no hob-nails in them at the time—and our suits still uninitiated to deluges of bacon-grease and a variety of what-not, perhaps they only thought us a couple of government men or Davy [Davey] Tree Surgeons.[2]

Once in North Adams, we went over to the "Berkshire Hotel,"[3] with packs on our backs. The desk-clerk eyed us rather suspiciously, asked for payment *in advance*, and called a surly bell-hop to show us to our room.

Like all hotel rooms in the summer, it was hot and stuffy, so we immediately went out to see the town. It was rather natural to be there owing to previous visits. While window-shopping, I overheard a fellow mention a dance and made up my mind to attend it as this would probably be the last chance for that sort of thing for some time. Jack was a bit tired so went back to the hotel and I hopped a bus for "Meadow Brook."

About one o'clock I stole into our room—Jack was wide awake, and why shouldn't he be? It was the night before the "glorious fourth." There was a store selling—or setting off—fire works just across the street. Some quiet individual in an apartment near the display had tuned in on a prize-fight, set the radio by the window, and through the courtesy of Western Electric, amplified the program in grand style. Well, fights, celebrations, and such, must end, so about three o'clock we actually did get to sleep.

JULY 4TH.   **Left Williamstown 7: A.M.**

Trail – 8 mi.

Arr. Seth Warner 4: P.M.

Jack and I had breakfast in North Adams and then took the bus to Williamstown. It was a grand morning and the prospects for a good first day on trail looked favorable. We walked from the center to the outskirts of the town and started our trail-work a few hundred yards from the rail road station. Until we reached the summit of Blueberry Mountain, it was mighty steep and rough going. While ascending a "rare" hillside, known as "Pine Cobble," we felt fatigue for the first time. It hit like a thunder-bolt. By some strange providence, its effects were short-lived, and you can rest assured that we were thankful for that.

By the time we reached the summit, it had begun raining and soon we were following indistinct blazes, scarcely visible through the mists. It was a strange sensation to be up there, for all practical purposes lost from the civilized world, and now and then, to hear the distant explosions of fire-works in the valley below, which was absolutely obscured under a bank of wandering mist.

We reached the Massachusetts–Vermont state line at 10:45 and, after a brief pause, pushed on through scrub growth, ferns, and bushes, which wet us through. It had stopped raining by then and the cool, fragrant, woods seemed welcome to us. Songs of birds, a gentle whispering breeze, and our footsteps, muffled by inches of leaf-mould, were the only sounds we heard. Seldom did we speak to break the impressiveness which surrounded us.

At 11:30 we stopped for lunch by a lumberman's camp—but which proved to be about a mile off the trail. While cutting the timber, they had cut the trees which bore blazes as well as others. The forest was a maze of winding paths, clearings, and logging roads. After lunch, we wandered about for over an hour, searching for the trail and finally, discovering an old woodchopper, were directed vaguely to it. What a satisfaction it was to find it again! It was like the joys experienced as a child when you find your way home after deciding to run away and seek your fortune like a fairy-prince.

About 2:30, we struck a wagon road just a little above the camp where we were to stay. By its side we saw a hunter's cabin and, noticing people there, made our way to ask them about the distance to Seth Warner. What a blessing followed!!!! The owner, Herr Krueger, seeing that we were tired (probably looking like the proverbial last rose of summer), took us in as if we had been his own sons. Such hospitality—we could not possibly have asked for more. Best of all, he gave us two quarts of German beer apiece, a place to stretch out and dry our clothes, and a hot dinner.

The last half-mile to camp was scarcely noticed and Jack—doggone't —I swear he didn't walk a straight line, nor possible could have. I staggered along behind him and know!

We arranged our things, had a nap and then returned to our German friends. By this time, the rest of the Krueger family had arrived—twelve in all—and they were staging a regular reunion, singing, telling stories, swapping friendly "gestures," and enjoying beer. Even the little children in arms sipped with their elders. There was no intoxication, no bawdy acts or words; what domesticity, what clean and honest fun our generation has lost!!!

Eventide approached, lengthening shadows crept across upland fields, a cool breeze swept across our faces—it was time for us to return to camp . . . . Darkness fell . . . . Our day was over, for on the trail, man lives by day.

JULY 5TH.   **Left Seth Warner 8:30 A.M.**
                                       Trail – 7 mi.
                                       Arr. Thendara 3:30 P.M.

We had an easy hike today and it surely seemed good. Everything seemed to be in our favor, just as yesterday nearly all turned against us.

The trail followed an old logging road most of the way and the grades were comparatively easy. It was a beautiful walk. For the most part we wended our way through woodland tracts which were moist and cool, and which were filled with a slightly musty odor, lending a primitive atmosphere to the surroundings.

Dropping from the ridge, the trail descended rapidly and skirted Sucker Pond—the reservoir and chief source of water for Bennington, Vermont. We stopped by this body of water for lunch—what a delightful spot! The reservoir is about a half of a mile in diameter and is surrounded by thick woods, in which the hard variety predominate. Its clear crystalline surface was slightly rippled and the inverted picture of the shore danced with a fascinating motion.

We stayed there about three hours and, after lunch, amused ourselves by enjoying the scenery, watching the fish which swam in numbers near the shore, and doing a bit of angling (not fishing). It was this way. We discovered a horn pout's[4] nest directly under the bank on which we were sitting. Each time we kicked the bank, two pouts would swim out and, after a few minutes, return to guard their young. Why, we asked ourselves, if we weighted a piece of mosquito-netting, and dropped it in front of the hole, couldn't we catch them as they swam out? — To make a long story short, we *did* catch "Frau" pout but "Herr" pout was too ellusive [*sic*], wise, or, what have you, to be stopped by such a base contrivance as we were using. — We must have looked like a couple of nit-wits angling in this manner, but it was a novel experience and gave us "that added something" for supper.

When we reached camp, we noticed immediately that we were in hedge-hog country. While I stayed inside to tidy up a bit, Jack went out to get clubs and, incidently [*sic*], to find out how the hunting prospects looked. Chance made me a better huntsman than he, for sitting in back of the stove, blinking blissfully, and looking most important, was friend porky himself. Shouting to Jack as I ran, I rushed through the door, found a club and returned, Jack following closely. Much to our disappointment, our "visitor" had checked out for parts unknown. Foiled at hunting, we shifted our attack on the flying wild-life which was thick—plenteee

Noticing that the stove pipe ended about a foot from its hole in the roof, we blocked up the hole with a stove-lid and started a smudge which would have been powerful enough to have taken care of ten such cabins. Our eyes smarted, tears ran from them, we coughed like a fellow smoking one of his father's cigars for the first time—but this was better than being eaten alive by midgets. The Indians used to call them "no-see-ums," and a few minutes in the cabin, prior to the smudge, convinced me that they were right.

About a quarter of a mile from the cabin was one of the nicest mountain-springs I ever hope to see. Indeed, it was a jewel. It rests close to the base of an old cedar, dampens moss on all sides, and quietly trickles over white and grey pebbles, then disappears again into the earth. Its waters are clear and cold and are flavored exquisitely with natural spices. We visited it as soon as we had arranged our temporary home, and lingered by it until nearly dusk.

We spent a peaceful evening enjoying the freshness of a cool breeze, lazily smoking, and watching the lights twinkling in the valley below. This was our first evening alone, our first intimate communion with nature, it shall never be forgotten.

JULY 6TH.   **Left Thendara 9:30 A.M.**
                                                      Trail – 7.5 mi.
                                            Arr. Bennington 12:30 P.M.
                                            Arr. Fay Fuller 3:15 P.M.

What a night we spent at Thendara! We had a match with two hedge-hogs; one was gnawing hell out of a board on the under side of Jack's bunk and the other, who was calmly chewing one of the camp settees, added a few more knotches [*sic*] to its already splintered edge. The latter left more quickly than he came and probably making a good deal more noise as Jack caught him amidships with a rock and knocked him clean off the bench.

After breaking camp, we trailed to the state road running into Bennington. The going was rather easy and again, the path led through cool, musty woods. About two miles from camp a doe crashed across the trail directly in front of us. It was an inspiring sight to see her gracefully bounding along with head up-raised, and the white on her tail bobbing in much the same way as a rabbit's does. Many gun for them in the fall, but I had rather hunt for them without a gun the year round. Hunting may be a great sport, but, unless for the sake of food, to proudly kill such a beautiful creature, seems almost like a crime.

On the way up Harmon Hill, just south of Bennington, we were pleasantly surprised to find an abundance of wild strawberries. We had a feast on them which was fit for the best of men. How many of them we ate I do not know but a long rest on top of the hill was welcome. A remarkable view of Bennington and the nearby valley was to be had from there. As we stood, with the wind literally swaying us on our feet, the sun was in such a position to make Bennington monument[5] stand out in a pencil-like silhouette, and the windows of many of the houses were transformed into so many glistening mirrors.

About quarter past twelve, we reached the road and, after leaving our packs at a farm near the trail, caught a ride to town with a good-natured motorist. Our first stop was at the post office. At that time we made our first contacts with home. I was a bit surprised not to find a letter from my beloved but as any schedule on the trail is a bit uncertain, such disappointment must be passed off lightly. The next move was to head for a barber shop—whether we needed tonsorial attention or not. The old codger made some remarkable transformations and we then dined at the "Paradise Café".[6] It may have been a mediocre place, perhaps the Greek proprietor hadn't shaved that morning, but it seemed mighty good to sit down at a table cloth and have a buxom wench trundle in the food. Shopping followed, after which we bummed back to the farm, picked up our packs and had a short hike into camp.

We met our first acquaintance on trail there—Ed Taylor, who owns a private camp about a half a mile from the Green Mountain lodge. He was a mighty likeable chap and we talked with him at length, leaving him to take a bath in a mountain brook. I have just one thing to say about that— it was cold, even the North Shore around Marblehead, Massachusetts, is a bath-tub compared with it. Just the same, after a day's hike, there's nothing like doing just that or, at least, bathing one's feet in a spring.

After our dip we cooked supper (two pounds of steak included) and then went up on the roof to watch the stars and enjoy our evening cigar. It was a joy to lie there, feel the cool breeze on our faces and listen to the roar of the mountain stream a few rods away.

———

JULY 7TH.   **Left Fay Fuller 9:30 A.M.**
                                      Trail – 6 mi.
                                      Arr. Glastenbury 1:00 P.M.

We had a grand night's rest and, after a hearty breakfast, broke camp. Everything was in tact [*sic*] except the sleeves of our sweaters on which one (or more) friendly field-mice did a surprising job. As we hiked along, the thought that we were climbing the first good sized mountain [Glastenbury] was constantly in our minds. It was a thrill to realize that the time had come when we should earnestly begin our ascents of the Green Mountains.

The trail up the mountain was in fine condition and, although the grade was steady, it only assumed a real serious nature for about a quarter of a mile. About a mile from the summit, we discovered two junco's nests within a few yards of each other. They were partially hidden in the grass which grew abundantly in the trail and were so cleverly concealed, that if we had not been stopping to rest at the time, we probably would not have found them. It was interesting to note how much of a racket the mother bird made as we walked over to look at them. Such a chatter; but it would have been cruel for us to have even thought of harming them in any way.

Only a few minutes before we reached the cabin it began to rain, needless to say, that little shack was a welcome sight. It was the first one which we had struck of steel construction. It is located about two hundred feet below the summit and has a fine southern exposure, although that feature didn't mean much as we were completely surrounded by clouds.

While we were getting in a supply of wood, the fire warden, who has a look-out and cabin at the summit, greeted us. After finishing camp duties, we spent the rest of the afternoon with Mr. Holbrook,[7] visiting

Family at Glastenbury Camp, 1933.
GMC photograph collection.

his shack, going up to the tower to see whatever view might be had—for
the rain had stopped and the clouds began to break by five o'clock—and
studying charts which he had of the section.

If the black flies were thick at Thendara, I don't know just how to
describe their numbers here. They existed in great droves and although
we put netting at the window of the cabin, did our best to keep the
door closed, and anointed ourselves with "dope," still they persisted
in getting into our hair, ears, and occasionally flew into our mouths.
(Perhaps this ought to have taught us a lesson to keep our mouths shut
when in a tight situation.)

We spent a quiet evening in our cabin except for one incident. Just
before turning in, we heard a scraping noise outside—could it be that
another porky wished to call on us? Arming ourselves with a couple of
clubs, we dashed out and turned our flashlight in the direction from
which the noise came. Not a hedge-hog but a friendly rabbit looked up
at us, blinked a few times, and then hopped away. Jack and I smiled at
each other and then went inside again.

JULY 8TH.   **Left Glastenbury 9:00 A.M.**
                                                  Trail – 10 mi.
                                           Arr. Grout Job 3:55 P.M.

When we awoke, clouds again surrounded us and a sprinkle of rain was falling. What a prospect for our longest journey since we left Williamstown!

Shouldering our packs, we started onward, waved goodby to the fire-warden, and pushed on through the mist. Before going far the heavens op'ed wide and then wider. I have seen it rain harder, but just when it was, or where, I cannot remember. A mile or two from the summit we stopped to put our ponchos around the packs and took the brunt of the storm ourselves; this would give us dry food and clothing when we reached camp (if we ever should, I thought).

We sloshed along. The incessant downpour soaked us to the skin. Our occasional songs seemed to drown in the falling ocean as soon as they sounded. The whole situation was so pathetic that it was funny. The water strained in from the outside while sweat oozed outward from the inside, and *all* the moisture trickled down into our shoes until they provided an ample, but uncomfortable pool for our feet to play in.

The trail lead us over many a hill and down more glades, and during the entire procedure, took no odds in attempting to reach a nearly perpendicular station. More than once we would slide down the steeper places, hoping for the best possible landing but knowing that whatever we did, the devil would take the hindermost.

About one o'clock we huddled ourselves under a poncho for lunch. Our festive board consisted of a few raisins to munch, apricots to chew on, and a couple of chocolate bars to increase our thirst. It was a cold and an extremely wet performance so we soon gave up the idea of eating as a bad one and pushed on. This wasn't such a wise plan either, for although we had not eaten much, the little which we had raised rumpus in Jack's stomach and we had to rest. It was impossible to find any place which might even approach dryness—we sat down where we were, Jack on a greasy mud bank, I on a rotten log which broke with my weight and gently set me into a miniature lake—oh well, what the hell!

About three o'clock the rain let up, although the frequent bogs provided many opportunities to put a little more water and mud into our shoes. There is one bog which I shall never forget. It was about twenty yards across, no detour was possible, we had to plough through it to the tune of sinking into the muck above the tops of our puttees at each step.

A half an hour passed. We reached the highway which runs through the pass in which the Grout Job is located. It was a beautiful sight, that muddy road, in comparison to the walking which we had had. After a mile of this easy going, we arrived at our destination looking, probably, like a couple of drowned rats and feeling damned uncomfortable.

We shared the Job, an abandoned lumber colony, with a group of boy scouts from New York state. It seemed good to have companions on the trail and especially after the day we had put in. The fellows were great visitors and we had a long talk with them after supper, sitting around a camp fire, enjoying our evening smoke, and looking at the stars which were now visible.

The boys went to bed rather early so their leaders, Mr. Graves and "Joe," accompanied Jack and me on a hunt for porcupines—any other wild life being an objective also. Our campaign took place in an old mill where we had noticed some enemies earlier in the afternoon. We did not have to search for very long before finding a large member of their clan meandering along in their characteristic rolling manner.—Gamely he died, boys, gamely he died!!—A double-barrel shot-gun fired at a distance of about twelve feet did the job, and what a job. The animal was not only killed, he was pulverized as well and his pieces were scattered all over the room in which we annihilated him.

What was next—a bit of fun for the boys who asked to be surely awakened if we shot anything. Returning to the barn, in which they were resting, we began a search for anything we might shoot. A good sized snake was found in one of the old horse-stalls . . . . Wham!!! and he shared a similar fate to that of the porky . . . . The hay-loft, where the boys were, was immediately in an uproar . . . . Wham!!! we sent a barn rat sprawling. Pandimonium [*sic*] broke loose upstairs and it was not very long before they all clambered down the ladder to see what the excitement was . . . . They were a bit disappointed not to find a porky, so sleepily climbed up again. We followed soon after and by ten o'clock, knew little more than they did . . . . Sleep was surely sweet that night!

JULY 9TH.   **Left Grout Job 8:40 A.M.**
Trail – 6 mi.(?)
Arr. Willis Ross 2:20 P.M.

We learned a bitter lesson today—never leave the LONG TRAIL for a suggested short cut.

After bidding our friends goodby, we started to follow an abandoned road from the Grout Job to Stratton Pond. This plan, which seemed feasible enough when explained to us by the warden on Glastenbury, might have eliminated the difficult ascent of Stratton Mountain, which has a wooded summit, thus affording little view, and, by the time saved, gained us nearly a day on trail time. The first hundred yards of the road were plain enough but then, all clearness changed to confusion. We should have turned back and taken the Long Trail but instead, took compass readings, sketched a path in our guide book, and pushed ahead through thick forest and heavy underbrush. Eternities seemed to pass. Flies were thick. Black flies were thicker. The bogs were all too plentiful. All in all, it was a mighty tough grind.

About quarter past one, we found the trail—the Long Trail—near the "Dufresne Job," another abandoned lumber settlement . . . . We sat down on the damp moss and breathed easily . . . . What a relief. I don't think that I was so glad to see the white blazes (with which the trail is marked) at this place as I was when we got lost the first day but, believe me, it was a mighty, mighty satisfying feeling to know that we were on the right track again.

We had scarcely left this spot when a thunderstorm, which had been rumbling in the distance for some time, ominously and gloomily rolled over the summit of Stratton Mountain. Jack and I doubled our pace. We arrived at the camp just as it started to rain. The heavens soon had op'ed, it was quite some distance to the next camp, so we decided to spend the rest of the afternoon there and get thoroughly dried out and have a good rest . . . . We built a roaring fire in the stove. Shoes made a peculiar sucking sound when they were drawn from our feet. Clothes, soaked by the wet, wandering, path in the strange woods, gave off a "quaint" odor. We did not mind. We were warm, had on dry garments, and a pot of coffee boiled joyously on the fire. Jack took a nap while I rummaged about and wrote letters home.

By half-past five I had supper coming along in fine shape, so awoke Jack and we had a grand meal—more than usual, as we knew that we would reach Manchester on the morrow. After eating, we took a paddle on Stratton Pond, which was right by the cabin although our boat was an unwieldy log raft. The beauties of the trip will never be forgotten.

The pond is about a mile long and, at its widest point, nearly a half a mile in breadth. As we slowly paddled the sun disappeared behind a fringe of trees which top the western hills. Its resplendant [*sic*] rays were caught by wisps of cloud above us and reflected in the water about us. A chorus of birds warbled their lullaby to the parting day. All nature seemed at perfect peace with mankind. A queer feeling of comfort and serenity pervaded my *self.* Toils of the day were forgotten: they seemed as if they had been experienced short ages ago and now, we were in some sort of a tranquil heaven on earth.

We did not go to bed as early as we customarily had, but sat up for a long while talking over all that had come to us on the trail and discussing our plans for the next few days . . . yet it wasn't such a very long while before we blew out the candles . . . all . . . all faded . . . sleep ensued.

JULY 10TH.   **Left Willis Ross 9:45 A.M.**

Trail – 9 mi.

Arr. Manchester 4:30 P.M.

Arr. LaChance's 6:00 P.M.

We had a wonderful night's rest and, after cleaning up the odds and ends of our food supply for breakfast, headed for Manchester, Vermont, as soon as the weather looked promising enough. The trail skirted the pond and then followed easy grades through hard-wood forests to Bourne [Bourn] Pond, an alleged haven for trout fishermen.

As the weather began to look dubious again, we did not stay at Bourne as long as I would have liked to but pushed on, following an abandoned logging rail road to the Buck Job, another deserted lumber camp, and Swesey Lodge. By this time, *of course*, it was raining again. A repetition of the hike from Glastenbury ensued. We sloshed along until about one o'clock and then ate lunch underneath ponchos. Water dribbled from our hats, softening the raisins which were dry and hard. We drank water ironically from our canteens—as if we were not wet enough already. We consumed our trail-beaten chocolate bars and again moved on.

Three miles from Manchester we arrived at Prospect Rock. While we stood on the promentory [*sic*], some strange power cleared the weather for about twenty minutes and we enjoyed a magnificent view of the valley below us. The town nestles at the foot of the dark green slopes of Mount Equinox. I wish that it were possible for me to describe the scene as we saw it.

Clouds soon obscured the view. A drizzle of rain, driven by a raw wind, descended . . . . We followed the "Rootville Road" into town, fortunately getting a ride after we struck the main highway.

As soon as we had purchased the necessary supplies for the next lap of our journey, we went to the Post Office—two wonderful letters from home were waiting for me. How happy I was to have them! It was worth all the hardships on the trail.

The distance from here to M. LaChance's place was travelled in style. We saw a taxi across the street and welcomed it like a long lost friend. My enthusiasm for the trail was no less then than at any time, in fact it has been increasing ever since leaving Williamstown, but it was a *real* pleasure to sit back in the car, listen to the swish of the water, *outside*, and watch the windshield wiper nonchalantly flicking the rain from the glass.

Our first stop was at Wells Dickinson's place, where hikers used to board, but the welcome sign no longer hung on the door. We followed the taxi driver's advice and put up at LaChance's, a tourists' camp which is located about three hundred yards from the trail. We had a full course dinner and then strained through the rain to our cabin and turned in, determined to stay there the next day if the rain continued—perhaps even if it was clear.

JULY 11TH.   **(A day at LaChance's.)**

We arose about half-past ten and, after a fine breakfast, which nearly assumed the proportions of our supper the night before, washed our clothes—whether they needed it or not. Within two hours, three good sized lines were domestically decorated with the "furnishings of our homes."

In the afternoon, we hitch-hiked into Manchester to do one or two errands which we had forgotten the previous day and returned to our hotel (ahem) a little before sunset. This small tourists' camp may be only another rather unattractive place for the hundred who rush over the mountain pass in their machines but it was a regular palace to us—including electric lights and, incidently, beer.

When we stopped at Wells Dickinson's the day before, we noticed a beautiful view of Stratton Mountain and the Glebe Range. Wishing to photograph them, we hiked up the road opposite the house—an elderly gentleman was sitting in a Dodge "beach-wagon" enjoying the scenery. He turned out to be a friend indeed.

It seems that he, Charles Earl, formerly was a business man in New York but ever since childhood had been a lover of Vermont. A few years ago, upon retiring from business, he bought an old farm on the Manchester–Peru road, and now lives there 'midst rural tranquility and the intimate handiworks of nature. How I envy him! After we talked with him for a few minutes, he offered to take us into Peru, suggesting a good country inn for supper. We accepted. Our surprise followed soon after we came onto town. He introduced us to Mrs. Russell, the proprietress of the "Russell Inn," and staked us to a typical Vermont meal.

We sat at the same table with a very charming family—the Woods. Their son Albert hoped to enter Dartmouth in the fall of 1931 but was refused admission. He is now in line for Syracuse. His sister Emily has been accepted at Skidmore where she will continue her work in music. It made me think of the years that Dottie spent at Wellesley to talk with her about counterpoint and composers which both had studied.

When we returned to Madame LaChance's she seemed a little peeved that we did not show up for supper but, upon paying our bill through the next morning's breakfast, she outwardly showed us that she felt much better. In fact, she sat with us for quite some time talking over her experience as a road-side hostess and hoping that we would spend a night at her camp if we were ever in that part of the country again.

Thus the evening passed. Ten o'clock found us in bed and ready for our next day's work on trail which, according to reports, was going to be a rare one.

View of Manchester from Prospect Rock, ca. 1910.
Courtesy of Vermont Historical Society.

JULY 12TH.   **Left LaChance's 8:30 A.M.**

Trail – 6 mi.

Arr. Mad Tom Camp 1:00 P.M.

A cold grey morning greeted us when we awoke. It was discouraging, after all the rain we had had on the trail, to push on again through more muck and gurry.[8] Some kindly spirit must have seen the disconsolate look on our faces for, before we had gone very far, the clouds broke and the prospects for a beautiful day turned up. As it turned out, the hike was by far the most pleasant one we had had on trail.

We reached the summit of Bromley Mountain a little before half-past eleven and climbed the observation tree[9] at the summit. The view from that point was superb. Monadnock was visible to the East, appearing like a faint grey ghost in the distance. The more intimate valleys and hills stood out in bold relief. As far as the eye could reach, nothing but a vast sea of hills was apparent. The majesty of the sight inspired us. We forgot past hardships while we revelled in present joys. The hills, which we were to cover for many days to come, reared their tree-topped heads before us. The adventures of past days lay to the south, pictured with shade and light effects which would have made the greatest painters ashamed.

We left Bromley a little after noon and it was not long before we reached Mad Tom Camp. Again, a porky-haven was before us. Jack looked at me and smiled. I glanced at him—we both smiled. Our heads nodded in common assent, we knew well what the night might bring forth. Never before in my life have I seen a more completely emaciated table. What was, was not, and what was not, was represented [*sic*] by grained and ragged gashes indescreetly [*sic*] gnawed.

The remainder of the afternoon passed rapidly. I puttered around the cabin doing odd jobs, cooked some "jello" and set it in the spring to jel [*sic*]. Jack wandered off a mile or so to see what prospects the brooks had for trout. There were none.

We spent the evening in visiting and reading the mail which we had received during the trip. As we turned in a deluge of rain drops played on the tin roof of the shack—a good-natured thunderstorm was in progress!

⊷

JULY 13TH.   **Left Mad Tom 9:00 A.M.**

Trail – 12.5 mi.

Arr. Black Branch 5:30 P.M.

After a wonderful night's rest we broke camp and ascended Styles Peak, a tough but interesting climb. The view from the summit was partially shut off by haze so we stayed only a few minutes and then crossed the "saddle" to Peru Peak. It was only a mile and a half in distance but it was the most difficult stretch which I have ever experienced.

A heavy wind of the preceding winter[10] had razed countless trees and sent them sprawling in all directions. It seemed to us as if the majority of them had found their resting place directly across the trail. Innumerable times it was a case of crawling beneath the windfalls or scrambling over them. Once in a while we would meet up with a problem of "double entente" where it was necessary to strain over one and, upon losing one's balance at its crest, dive underneath another a few feet away. I got caught between the two, in one of those choice situations and, suspended by my pack which was too bulky to pass through, wriggled and squirmed for what seemed hours. To give the scene added zest, Jack stood along the trail a few rods and laughed ironically at me—perhaps his guffaws were not all ironic but that is of little importance. In plain language, the crossing was hell.

After an hour and a half we reached the wooded Peru Peak. We had had enough of trees to last us for some time so we immediately proceeded. The trail from this point was a blessing, following easy slopes down the northwest side of the ridge. In a short time we arrived at Buffum Pond (or Griffith Lake) where we had lunch and rested for over an hour. Jack made his way out to a rock a few yards from shore and tried a bit of casting. His labors were rewarded by great quantities of lily pads, lilies, weeds, and an astounding absence of fish.

Eames fishing at Griffith Lake.
Courtesy of Hindes family.

The trail from here to Griffith Camp was very beautiful and comparatively easy. It ran along a flood-washed mountain road which parallels the course of Roaring Brook, a band of foam which leaps and bounds over a rocky bed. The hike along this section was not without an amusing incident. One of our co-habitants, a porcupine, who was evidently out for an afternoon stroll, greeted us as we rounded one of the bends in the road. We stopped short and dug out our cameras, hoping to photograph him. No photographer ever had a tougher job in arranging his subject for a sitting. Our friend absolutely refused such publicity and immediately headed for a pile of rocks near the spot. I did my best to make him understand that we meant him no harm but the critter's obstinance [*sic*] was not a thing to be meddled with. After much vain persuasion to make him face the camera, Jack gave him a powerful kick and sent him sprawling some five or six feet beyond. He squealed a bit then lay quite still. Compassion got the best of us and we clubbed him to death and set about to de-quill Jack's boot which looked like a Christmas tree after New Year's Eve. We drew forty-one miniature spears, which were securely embedded by their barbs, out of his shoe.

A little after three o'clock we arrived at the abandoned lumber settlement Griffith and located the Green Mountain Club shelter, only to find a healthy and actively inhabited wasps' nest hanging from the ridgepole. As the day had been beautiful, we decided to push on until about supper-time and camp in the open. After a two-hour walk we reached the Black Branch River and found an ideal camping spot in a hard wood grove. We ate a light supper and, after sitting by our camp-fire for an hour or so, retired. The stars, great hosts of them, blinked above our heads. Our packs swayed gently from the branch of a tree where we had hung them.

<hr />

JULY 14TH.   A day at Griffith.

Just before midnight of the thirteenth it started raining great dogs—gawd! It was a marvel to feel it pour in such quantities. To make a long story short, as soon as it was light enough for us to see the blazes, we retraced our steps to Griffith and put up at a fern-picker's cabin.[11] We awoke him by loud knocking and shouting at the door. After some time we heard him coming—he opened the door—bleary eyes, a yawn, and a passive smile, greeted us—we streamed inside. I don't think that I have ever welcomed a set of dry clothes so much as I did on this occasion—even that memorable trip from Glastenbury cannot compare with it. There, at least, it was day time, here, we became soaked during a gloomy night with no hope of improving our situation until dawn, until we had hiked some miles, carrying packs, having had no food for some time, and even then facing the chance that everything in our packs would be soaked. They were not.

Warmth of a fire.

Coffee and griddle-cakes.

Human companionship.

A brighter day dawned and we were happy again.

The weather cleared off about seven o'clock. Jack went out fishing with "Shotgun," as our new found friend called himself, while I stayed behind to do the chores. I finished them about the middle of the morning and then communed with my beloved.

A little after eleven o'clock the fishermen returned. What a return!!! They brought back a mess of twenty-five trout for lunch. It was almost worth the hardships of the night before to have such a feed as that. It wasn't very long before we had eaten them and crawled into bed for a much needed rest.

After our nap, "Shotgun" took us to a small hunting camp which was located near the trail and, much to our astonishment, was not over three hundred yards from the place where we had attempted to sleep the preceding night. He stayed with us until after supper and then went back to his camp with a cronie [*sic*] of his who showed up on the scene about half past six.

Evening approached. Shadows of night crept ominously into the valley. The last embers of the fire in the stove dwindled. We slept. Far off in the country towns clocks were striking eight but we did not hear them.

JULY 15H.   **Left Hunting Lodge 7:30 A.M.**
                                                            Trail – 15.5 mi.
                                           Arr. Roskeney Farm 4:30 P.M.

This exceptionally long day on the trail was necessary as our food supply ran low on account of the day lost at Griffith. We realized the nature of the work cut out for us but as we were sure of a comfortable farm to stay in at night, determined to undertake it no matter what happened.

The trail was unusually picturesque and, on the whole, did not prove difficult. The first few miles led us through birch forests to Little Rock Pond, a gem set in a verdant paradise of loveliness. From thence easy grades took us to the summit of White Rocks Cliff, which is eight miles from East Clarendon.

The view from this point of vantage was magnificent. The southern

Roskeney Farm, East Clarendon, 1932.
GMC photograph collection.

end of the Otter Creek Valley stretched its narrow levelness at our feet. Practically surrounding it a panorama of rugged peaks lifted their shoulders. They ranged all the way from the Coolidge Range, directly opposite us, to Killington on the right; from the Taconic range at one angle, to the ghosts of the Adirondacks lying far to the northeast. Although we had covered less than half the distance from camp to the farm, we remained there for some time enjoying the natural splendor.

From the beginning of the trip our policy had been to get the most out of scenic marvels. As time has gone on, we have become more and more certain that that is the only method to hike the trail. Those who rush along attempting to set records, those who are a bit afraid to come into camp an hour later than they had planned, lose the very heart of the trail. How nature can mean a great deal to them is beyond my powers of reason. Let roaring trains, straining automobiles, and soaring airships—all handy, convenient inventions—accomplish extraordinary feats of speed, but let me wander through the mountains and feast on the beauties which abound on every side!!

From White Rocks, the trail dropped steeply to the old Bulley Farm, crossed the Wallingford–East Wallingford road, and then climbed earnestly onto a ridge, passing Buffum Camp where we rested for lunch.

A short time afterwards the heavens did their usual opening stunt. We plodded up Button Hill. It was some button! Leaving this height the trail wandered along what seemed to be an endless ridge. Although it had stopped raining, the trees were dripping wet and the mushy humus beneath our feet again provided miniature pools in our shoes. Finally the descent into Clarendon Gorge began and the altitude which we lost in the ensuing mile was astonishing.

A little after four o'clock we reached the Rutland–Bellows Falls highway and soon strained into the Roskeney Farm tired and wet. Vermont has always been famous for its hospitality but on this occasion it was more welcome than ever, especially to Jack whose feet were swollen with seven blisters. The last miles must have been extremely painful for him and the courage which he showed during them, pluckily hiking, constantly smiling, is worthy of a great deal of praise . . . . What a difference a *hot bath* and a home-cooked supper made!

We went into Rutland that evening to the movies and had a spree all by ourselves. It seemed good to enjoy such entertainment after being away from civilization for two weeks. We met Wess Taylor[12] '31, and Ed Marceau[13] '34, Dartmouth friends, at the show and had a good visit with them afterwards, and made plans for Ed to meet us on Killington on the seventeenth.

JULY 16TH.   **Left Roskeney 11:00 A.M.**

Trail – 6.5 mi.

Arr. Mrs. Balch's 3:00 P.M.

We arose much refreshed by the home-like care which we received at Roskeney's but, due to the bad condition of Jack's feet, decided to take an easy day on the trail. As things turned out, I am glad that we did for the hike proved one of the loveliest which we had had since we left home.

There was nothing spectacular about it, but the beautiful quietness of it all made a deep impression on me.

To begin with, it was a glorious day; so clear, so cool, so grand. There was nothing which could possibly destroy the perfect harmony between us and nature. The woods, fields, all was robed exquisitely and everything surrounding us seemed bubbling over with life.

After hiking for a little over two hours, we reached the Frank Smith farm in the township of Cuttingsville. I say township, for the farm might as well have been forty miles from the settlement instead of seven, as far as appearances disclosed. Jack and I both received mail at this point. Mine was from Dottie.

A bit further on, the trail broke into a clearing. Killington stood out before us massively. It was majestic. Its presence made you feel both great and small: great, in that you possessed as much as any human can of nature's wonders; small, because that which you possessed was such a small portion of all which surrounded you.

An hour and a half more brought us to our destination, a typical Vermont farm, owned by charming people. They were real honest-to-goodness folk, attractive by virtue of their simplicity and frankness. Not the slightest sign of artificiality could be detected in their character.

After supper, two hikers came off the trail, having journeyed from Killington. We sat around until late swapping stories about the trail and enjoying the companionship of others who are mountain enthusiasts.

———•———

JULY 17TH.   **Left Mrs. Balch's 9:00 A.M.**
                                     Trail – 6 mi.
                         Arr. Killington 1:00 P.M.

Today, we climbed the first of Vermont's "big three"—Killington. It was a grand climb and very beautiful.

For the first three miles the trail followed a delightful mountain stream—ascending gently, wandering completely. We wondered when the trail would settle down to business. Our minds were not in that state for a very long period.

We turned sharply to the left. A steep grade ensued which continued until the shoulder of the mountain was reached. As we worked our way upwards, small stones, loosened by our feet, scurried downward. Now and then, a branch would break off as we grasped it for support and its breaking would scare some feathered wild thing which would zoom skyward, uttering warning that man approached. They had nothing to fear. The days on trail had made us quite as natural as they.

Soon after reaching the main ridge, the peak came in view for the first time. Its rocky head loomed above the timber, which lay scattered a few hundred feet below. It stood out clearly, nearly touching a fringe of cloud and seemingly piercing the sky.

We worked forward. In another hour we reached the steel cabin which is about a quarter of a mile from the summit and about a hundred yards from the new stone shelter. I smiled to myself and recalled the first time I prepared a meal within the older place. I was cooking flap-jacks. One of them stuck to the frying pan a little more tenaciously than usual. I gave it a sharp jerk. Exit the pan-cake. It slowly soared from the pan and disappeared through the stove-pipe hole in the roof. Oh well, what of it? I successfully cooked another.

Anxious to reach the summit, we climbed to "Porky Lodge." Soon after our arrival (and as soon as a shower had passed) we scrambled to the peak. A keen wind struck our faces. The dark storm clouds scurried southward.

It seemed as if the world was beneath our feet. Rolling hills and broad valleys could be seen on all sides. Far to the north, and shrouded in a blue-grey mist, rose Le Lion Couchant,[14] Mount Mansfield, and the Jay Peaks—future "worlds to conquer," especially the Jays. They are the most northern of the Green Mountains. From them the trail continues to the Canadian border, only eight miles distant. We could see the Adirondacks to the northwest and a summer's sun slowly dropping to meet them. A long silvery ribbon tinged with old rose, flashed the sunset back to us. It was Lake Champlain. How natural, how close to home and my dreams that body of water made me feel!

We dropped below for supper and were joined by Eddie Marceau and two of his friends. We spent a quiet evening together and then turned in. As we looked into the Otter Creek Valley, we could see the lights of Rutland and numerous country towns. They seemed ghostly.

—————

JULY 18TH.   **Left Killington 11:00 A.M.**
Trail – 5.5 mi.
Arr. Long Trail Lodge 12:40 P.M.

We bade goodby to Eddie. After breakfast and a visit with the fellows at "Porky Lodge" we left for Sherburne Pass, intending to ascend Pico Mountain if the weather permitted.

The trail was in wonderful condition, our packs were light, so we swung along carelessly, making exceptionally good time. An hour's run, and much of the time was spent in travelling that way, brought us to Pico Camp which is located on the northern slope of the mountain bearing that name.

The only shower bath along the Green Mountain Club trails is located here. Did I say a shower? There is a stockade a few rods from the cabin into which water from a nearby spring has been piped along a grooved log. The water flows from the end of said log, splatters on another log, and there you have it. The structure is rustic to the nth degree and the water—well, it is rustic also.

We met some folks near the cabin who were hiking to Killington. They were enthusiastic. The men carried box lunches. It seems strange to see people in "civilian" clothes on the trail. They seemed very much impressed by the fact that we were headed for the Canadian border and stopped long enough for us to strike up a pleasing acquaintance.

We soon left them and within the next half-hour, reached the Long Trail Lodge. Its construction is unique and its beauty unparalelled [*sic*]. I feel as though the words of Jim Taylor, the father of the Long Trail, come as near describing the lodge as is possible. "The beauty of the autumn woodland is in the house itself. Above dark grey rafters of maple, and hanging over is the bright lacy bark of silver birches like mistle-toe, a veritable woodsy place, and in every nook are wrought dainty designs with twig and branch and root as delicately as though architect Thayer[15] were a worker in gold and platinum and precious stones." I cannot add more than to say, if you wish to understand rustic art in its highest form, visit this place—but not hastily.

As soon as we had registered we went to our room, stopping for a few moments on the porch to chat with two people from Winchester. I was surprised to find Miss Monroe and her cousin, Mr. Fletcher, there. Near our room we noticed a sign "Shower Bath." I looked at Jack and he at me. He scratched the small of his back . . . . We took the first hot shower since home. Home, how distant that place seemed!

We ate dinner, a chicken dinner.

I left to visit Camp Sangamon[16] about an hour afterwards. It is a summer camp for boys located about twenty miles from the pass and where I spent many months several years ago. Motorists were kindhearted

Living room, Long Trail Lodge.
GMC photograph collection.

and I arrived a short while after supper.

Yes, it seemed good to be back there again. I ate a large meal with the director, Mr. Leon [Leone] E. Smith, and mingled with the fellows until taps. At that time I histed [hoisted] myself into an upper bunk.

JULY 19TH.   **At the Long Trail Lodge.**

I stayed at the camp until chapel service was over and then returned to join Jack, stopping to do a few errands in Rutland on the way back. It seemed good to rest on the piazza of the Lodge again. The hot city streets, which I had paced a few hours before, were easily forgotten and I was aware of nothing but the coolness and quietness of the mountains.

It was a beautiful day and many tourists were about. They all tried to appear strong. Men would strike their cramped chests. Awkward women in homely knickers strode about—why didn't they remove their cosmetics? I laughed to myself and rested my feet on the porch railing.

This afternoon I became acquainted with a most remarkable man— Mr. Erickson.[17] At first sight he might easily be taken for an eccentric tramp, a sort of curiosity, a hermit which one reads about in books but never meets face to face. His hair hung in folds from the center of his head and broke on his shoulders. His beard, meticulously kept, reached his collar bones. He wore a khaki suit and a leather jerkin.[18] His boots were heavily hobbed but did not scuff when he walked.

A few minutes of conversation changed my whole opinion of the man. He was no longer a strange person. No longer did I look at him and feel like turning to anyone near me and talk about him in a low voice; that was not the case.

I became deeply interested in the sincere and yet mysterious personality of the man. He talked simply but not wholly freely. I learned a wonderful philosophy from him but discovered little about the man himself.

He is a native of Denmark but has been absent from that country for a number of years. He is now an American citizen. Strangely enough, he has never returned to his native land. Some secret event exiled him—but not from other parts of Europe. He has travelled it afar; from the slopes of Mont Blanc to the wilds of Northern Siberia where he spent three lonely years. A revolver was his companion at the time.

During the World War he served in the Allied forces and since then has wandered throughout the Eastern United States. Although he signs his name as, Erickson, Carmel, New York, his home is nature; in his own words, "Wherever I may be." He is an inhabitant of the out-of-doors which harbors men of every creed and nationality, which begins at the end of thronging and ends with the haunts of daring explorers.

Mr. Erickson, i.e. Eiler Larsen.
Courtesy of Hindes family.

Mr. Erickson is a man and a social order. He loves the smile of children, the warmth of occasional conversation, but above all, Nature. His philosophy seems simple. It is founded on Plato, a book of whom he carries constantly in his pack.

He has not always been a man of the tranquility of which he spoke. For some time he was a banker of Wall Street. He possessed quite a reputation at the time and was known as "the flower of Wall Street." His stay did not exceed three years. Nature called him. He answered.

At present he is hiking over mountain trails from Mt. Katahdin in Maine to southern Georgia, covering the White and Green mountains enroute [*sic*]. His livelihood is earned by occasional lectures. His ambition is to set down his life for the benefit of others—it will be a noble work.

His farewell to us was, "Best of luck. We shall meet again in the Himalayas. God bless you, my boys."

JULY 20TH.   **Left Long Trail Lodge 10:00 A.M.**
Trail – 12.5 mi.
Arr. Carmel Camp 8:10 P.M.

We bade Mr. Erickson farewell. Our spirits were high and the weather was low as we started on our way.

Jack's stomach, which had bothered him quite a bit on the trail, began to kick up after the first mile. It didn't help the looks of our prospects at all. I can not figure out just why he has so much trouble. We had had a fine rest after breakfast, as on many other mornings, had taken the first mile slowly—yet here it was, all knotted up. We rested. Pushed on at a moderate pace. Things seemed to be going better. We quickened our pace.

Just before the Noyes Pond Shelter we met two fellows clearing trail. We stopped with them, asking the conditions of the trail. They assured us that everything was all fine as far as Carmel. I'd like to see them again and tell them that their idea of a good trail differs considerably from mine!

Noyes Pond was the spot where we ate lunch. It is beautiful there. We rested for over an hour. There was a bird in a tree nearby whose incessant chatter broke a possible stillness. Just as we were to leave, thunder rolled ominously to the south-east. In spite of the warning, we shouldered our packs.

What a couple of nit-wits we were. In just about a half hour after leaving the heavens op'ed. Down she came with plenty of sound effects. It's surprising how thunder will echo back and forth in the mountains. The sound seems to come from all sides and linger awhile. To make matters worse, the condition of the trail became increasingly rotten and the grades became appreciably steeper. There are few instances on trail which provide more difficulties than a trail of wet humus which follows sideslopes diagonally. Such was our course for the next five miles.

The trail swung alternately from the east to the west side of the ridge from which Mount Carmel rises. I had made up a little melody. I sang it constantly. It helped me to trudge along. I was wet, tired, hungry. Jack was too. We didn't find out until later because a fellow doesn't feel much like talking under those circumstances.

At six o'clock we arrived at a deceiving junction. Blazes were scarce. Once clear signs lay splintered on the ground. Alternately we wandered from the spot. It was getting darker. A half an hour passed. We found the trail and as we smiled to each other little trickles of water coursed the wrinkles in our cheeks.

Hardly able to put one foot in front of the other, we pushed on. It was darker now. I sang my little song, but had to stop in the middle of it. Image being out of breath, huh! . . . In another hour it was dark. Our pace became necessarily slower. We oozed along in the muck. We crawled over slippery rocks. The clouds were low and our flashlights made little impression on them.

It was eight o'clock. Jack and I leaned on each other and sighed for relief. "Carmel Camp .2 mi.," we read . . . . Ten minutes passed . . . We entered the little steel shack. We sat down on a box; a pool of muddy water formed by our boots.

I lit a fire and set some soup to heat, then changed my clothes . . . . The soup boiled . . . . We drank . . . . We stumbled into bed.

JULY 21ST.   **A day at Carmel Camp.**

We awoke about nine o'clock. It was too wet to push on and we were too tired to face eleven miles.

Our general program was rest and plenty of it. Welcome it was.

A little after lunch we climbed to the summit [Mount Carmel] but were forced to return as it began to rain again.

It was still raining when we went to bed a little after eight. Distant thunder rumbled.

JULY 22ND.   **A day at Carmel Camp.**

"Din!" I awoke. Jack was calling me; said that his stomach was off on another rampage. We decided to stay over another day. Jack fell asleep again.

I got up, cooked a little breakfast and then started down the mountain to New Boston.[19] Yes, there are three farms there. One of the men drove me to Chittendon [Chittenden] from where I phoned father and got in touch with a local doctor. It made me feel lots more easy.

Following their advice, I bought some fresh farm products and borrowed some Milk of Magnesia from the "oldest resident." Kindly old soul, she; her days were spent in smoking a pipe, fidgetting with knitting, and scolding her great-great grand-daughter. I listened to her wild tales of the frontier . . . . It was time to return.

A Mr. and Mrs. Borne, from Winchester, Massachusetts, happened along and took me as far as the beginning of the trail in their car.

Jack came along nicely. We built a rustic "seat" for the cabin and cleared a trail to it. Probably the porkies will have it all chewed to pieces by next spring.

Towards evening Jack seemed so much better, that I decided to go down to the farm-house for supper. What a meal. There is nothing like a feed prepared by a country wife to perk a fellow up. After supper I went out on the piazza and visited with the hired man and "his boss" . . . . An angry bellow came from the pasture . . . . All three of us started out to round up the bull but I took the boss' advice and hit the trail . . . . I could hear the critter yawlin' for some distance.

Jack had gone up to the summit to watch the sunset. It was glorious. The sun was dropping behind the Adirondacks. Every cloud, on both horizons, was tinged with color. The lake, at the foot of the western mountains, looked like a bloody ribbon. We would be able to watch the sun dye Champlain for many evenings to come.

I thought of home. I dreamed of ideals. I wondered how a man could witness such a view and not feel a little closer to God. I wondered how one could keep from thinking of all that was dear to him and if he was in love, how such natural splendor could fail to rouse his desire to be with her.

Darkness soon followed. A biting wind chilled us. We wended our way back to camp and built a fire. How differently we felt from the night before last!

———•———

JULY 23RD.   **Left Carmel Camp 8:30 A.M.**
                                                        Trail – 10.7 mi.
                                        Arr. J. S. Hooker's (Brandon) 2:00 P.M.

Jack felt considerably better when we got up this morning and we started off with high spirits for Hooker's place. As the day progressed whatever clouds there were in the morning, cleared. The sun was hot, but as most of the trail followed logging roads, shade protected us from it.

As the trail skirted the north-western slopes of Carmel and Bloodroot mountains, we could see many views of Lake Champlain and the Otter Creek Valley. At those times we often watched an automobile, at any rate a moving speck, crawling along, and wondered if the occupants were enjoying Vermont as much as we.

We reached Bloodroot Gap about noon, a natural cut of great size and beauty. From that point the DuVal trails[20] run to Brandon. We went down a short distance to take photographs from the top of a cliff.

The trail followed a well-defined logging road from Bloodroot Gap. The grades were easy and we fairly ran along. We reached the Sunrise Camps about one o'clock and stopped for lunch. There is one of the most beautiful rustic bridges I have ever seen near the camps. In fact, it is one of the few bridges which have been provided to cross mountain streams. Our usual procedure had been to balance across a felled tree or wade the blamed thing.

We only rested for a few minutes at Sunrise and then pushed on to the Brandon–Rochester Pass and Hooker's farm. Letters were waiting for us, the first since the Long Trail Lodge, and we read them eagerly. Mine was from my fiancée. After unpacking, which consisted of spreading out all of our possessions on a feather bed, we hitch-hiked into Brandon.

Signpost at Brandon Gap.
GMC photograph collection.

We dropped post cards to the folks and were careful to mention that we had had haircuts. As the afternoon was still young, we walked out and visited the abandoned marble quarries.[21] All that there is left, are three awful holes partially filled with water. The once glittering sides are weather-beaten. Rusty hoists sprawl on the ground. The iron rail around the holes is also rusty and sways when you touch it.

We ate supper in town and then went to a show. By this time our clothes had had their initiations so that the folks about us moved over a seat from us. I wonder what they thought the matter was.

After the show, we went back to Hooker's, walking most of the way. It was a six mile hike to Goshen and although we were tired, found time to have a midnight lunch, and to write letters.

JULY 24TH.   **Left Hooker's 9:45 A.M.**
                                    Trail – 7.5 mi.
                                    Arr. Sucker Brook 3:30 P.M.

After an old-fashioned Vermont breakfast we left the farm, Mr. Hooker Jr. driving us to the top of the pass [Brandon Gap] in his car. We had been climbing for only a few minutes when Jack remembered that he had left some of our food supply at the farm—two miles behind. We passed a few remarks. I left him whittling on a maple twig. There were no kind-hearted motorists driving the pass. I returned to Jack an hour later, all out of breath. He had finished some sort of a spoon affair that he said would be useful. I had my doubts about it.

Great Cliff of Mount Horrid, 1912.
Courtesy of Vermont Historical Society.

We scrambled to the summit of the Mount Horrid cliffs. The state highway lay below us, some six or seven hundred feet; we wondered how much we would splash if we fell off the cliff. People do imagine those sort of things. A cloud of dust—a very small cloud—preceded by a speck ascended and descended the pass—we wondered if that car boiled. It would have not been the first one.

From the cliffs the trail ascended to the summit of the mountain and then continued in a northwestern direction. Three mountains separated us from the camp: Cape Lookoff, White Rocks, and Romance. The views from their sparsely wooded summits interested me considerably. Points in the Champlain Valley and many on the lake itself could be discerned if you knew where to look for them—I did. The sight of a small pond just north of Brandon, I cannot recall the name, reminded me of the time mother and I had lunch by it. It was a hot afternoon. A New York–Montreal bus came in, the driver ordered a hot-dog from "Kate." She handed him the dog; he slapped her on the back and called her an old fool. Mother didn't know just what to make of it. When she remarked to her helper that she was going to "Montry" with the fellow some day, I didn't know just what to make of it either.

We met a group of boys from Camp Kewaydin[22] on trail. They were eating lunch. We stopped and munched with them. They were young boys. The majority had never been on trail before and they had an inquisitive air about them. They seemed to ask countless unspoken questions of their leaders and us. Being with them reminded me of the trips I took at Camp Sangamon when I was a boy. Camp Sangamon, that was the place where I made my first real contact with the Green Mountains.

We left them a little after one o'clock and after an easy hike, reached camp. The cabin, built of peeled logs, was in perfect harmony with the surroundings. It is located in a birch glade. It rests close beside a stream which babbled constantly; the babbling seemed to almost speak to us as we rested that evening.

JULY 25TH.   Left Sucker Brook 9:45 A.M.

                                            Trail – 7 mi.

                                            Arr. Boyce Lodge 5:30 P.M.

Just before breakfast, a rip-roaring thunder storm hit camp. They aren't so bad if you can be on the inside looking out but when you are trying to cook a meal on an open fire-place, the situation is slightly different. The bacon sizzled in a pan which steamed and sputtered when the rain hit it. The pan-cakes were a complete failure. We tried to make some but, after only producing a couple of soggy sponges, gave it up as a bad job. We contented ourselves with eating grape-nuts with water on them. Lord knows there was enough of that around!

By nine o'clock the rain had stopped and after waiting nearly an hour for the water to stop dripping off the trees, we sploshed [*sic*] along. We climbed Mount Worth, which is located a short distance from camp. The level places of the trail were mud and the steeper places were masses of wet pine needles. It was grand! Every time you took a step, the goo gave you a "Bronx cheer." As we neared the summit, the mud grew less and rocks more plentiful. In another hour we reached the Lake Pleiad lookout. The clouds had lifted. Breadloaf Mountain stood out clearly to the north. The lake lay below us like a jewel. We could just barely distinguish folks moving on the shores. When we reached the lake, we discovered that they were students from the Middlebury Summer School on a picnic.

Another two hours carried us through a second thunder storm and brought us to the Breadloaf Inn. We thought of the picknickers and wondered if the whole gang of them were able to get into the small shelter [Lake Pleiad Lodge] near the lake. The guide book says that it will accommodate twelve. Well, in a storm, trail shelters seem to have a faculty of growing.

Upon applying for a room at the Inn, I was told that it was full. If it was full, that was the first time in years. The clerk seemed anxious to sell us provisions and send us on our way. I made up my mind to drive up there later in the summer and apply for a room. Civilian clothes might made a difference. Clean trail clothes might have made a difference then. Who knows???

Jack and I pushed on to Boyce Lodge over the Burnt Hill trail. Every time we tired from the climb, we would sit down and curse the clerk who told us the Inn was full.

—————

JULY 26TH.   **Left Boyce Lodge 8:00 A.M.**

Trail – 17 mi.

Arr. Battell Lodge 7:00 P.M.

This was surely a day of days on the trail but it proved to be one of the best. We were both pleasantly surprised in not being too tired at its close.

The day itself was condusive [*sic*] to a long hike. It was mildly warm. A breeze wandered southward. The air was clear. The hills and valleys stood out in bold relief each time we could look off.

A few hours hiking carried us to the summit of Breadloaf Mountain. The trail was fine; every turn of it brought a new experience to us whether scenery or glimpses of animal life. A rustic tower on the peak lifted us above the trees. From this point we reviewed the hikes of many past days. Many shoulders loomed to the East—they were the cliffs of the Vermont presidentials. The next few miles led over them. Far to the northeast, the presidentials of the White Mountains made a saw-tooth horizon. From our angle, Mount Washington looked smaller than the rest. Lake Champlain stretched to the West. The Adirondacks in back of Westport, New York, were especially prominent. There was the sharp peak of Marcy and the rounded dome of Whiteface. A pale of smoke hung over the blast furnaces at Port Henry.[23]

We descended. We scrambled over the presidentials. The saddle between Wilson and Cleveland mountains was like the one between Styles and Peru peaks. Hundreds of trees sprawled across the trail. We had to climb standing trees often, sight the general direction of the trail and hit for it by detours which were better than the blazed route—at least we thought that it must be blazed somewhere.

We arrived at Cooley Glen Lodge about one-thirty. It was a wreck. The only part of it which was not either half or totally destroyed was the metal roof and the supporting beams. Everything else was scattered hither and yon. It looked as if a bear had chased another animal—perhaps a bob-cat—around the stove and through one of the walls. We rested for an hour and a half and then ascended Grant. The trail was moderately steep but climbed through country which had been razed by forest fire. Stubble, stumps, and loose rocks were too plentiful for comfort.

Our trip for the summit to the Lincoln–Warren Pass [Lincoln Gap] was uneventful. We walked rapidly or ran most of the way. I was travelling at a rapid pace when I hit a bog. My feet went out from under me. I slid along my nether cheeks for some ten yards. Jack said I looked like a steam plough. I didn't feel like one. I felt like hell.

It was six o'clock. We had rested a half an hour at the pass. Over fourteen miles of trail lay behind us. Two more still remained and in that two miles, there was a thousand feet to climb. Just before we started, a car boiled over the pass. We wondered if that was the way we'd feel after an hour or so.

It was dusk when we reached the cabin. A fire burned in the stove. Food was simmering in kettles at the back. We drank some of the coffee and put some of our own on. The party blew in in about a half an hour. There were four couples from New York. We let the women do the rest of the cooking and helped the men arrange camp for the night. It seemed good to have company in camp, especially after the day we had put in. There is something which is just about perfect in sitting by a camp fire and quietly talking and smoking after you have had a wearisome day and haven't seen but a few persons for days on end.

We visited until nearly three o'clock in the morning. During the last two hours, we played poker on a bough bunk. I was glad when the game was over. The light by which we played came from a number of candles which we had set on a board on the boughs. They seemed steady enough but if they had ever tipped over, it would have been too bad for the new lodge, the surrounding woods and our belongings, which were well scattered about.

JULY 27TH.   **Left Battell 8:30 A.M.**
Trail – 11.8 mi.
Arr. Frank Beane's 4:30 P.M.

Haze, rising from overheated valleys, shut off views which would have been grand had the air been clear. It was a disappointment as we were now travelling the famous Monroe Skyline of the Long Trail. Waiting for a clear day was out of the question. Our food supply was running low. We pushed on. The trip along the highest ridge of the trail went for nought [*sic*] as far as seeing anything was concerned. We walked rapidly, crossing over the peaks of Nancy Hanks, Lincoln, and Ellen mountains.

We stopped for some time on this last peak. It had been a rigorous five miles. While we were there two porkys entertained us by scratching and clawing their way up a stunted tree. Every once in a while they would stop, chatter to one another and then munch away at a piece of bark. They didn't pay much attention to us. A few blinking glances—that was all. We named them Sal and Hal and left them to figure out a christening for themselves.

We stopped at Glen Ellen Lodge for lunch and then tackled General Stark Mountain. The descent IS sumpin'. After meandering on a slight ridge the trail fell. It twisted and turned. It shot down some ledges and skirted others, narrowing to inches in many places. It reached Dean's Cave and squeezed through it, plunged downward, and if you weren't skidding on your feet, you did a circle or two before your backsides struck the ground. We reached the Appalachian Gap and sat down—for a rest.

It was three o'clock. Baby and Molly Stark mountains sheered upwards before us. Birch Glen Lodge was on the other side of them. We left the trail proper and followed the Gap to the Hanksville–Starkboro [Starksboro] road. An abandoned road leads through the gap. I don't think that it has been used for the past forty years.

There was mail waiting for us at Frank Beane's place.

After a visit with the Beanes Jack and I went to bed. It was hot and stuffy in the bed room. We slept in the same bed but could hardly see one another—a soft but prominent ridge of feathers billowed between us. Gawd, but it was hot!!!

JULY 28TH.   **Left Frank Beane's 8:35 A.M.**
                                  Trail – 9.3 mi.
                      Arr. Montclair Glen Lodge 5:10 P.M.

We returned to the Long Trail by an approach trail from the West. Birch Glen Lodge is at the junction—a beautiful cabin standing in a

grove of silver birches and close to a talkative stream. The stove is in good condition. The bunks are firm and there is a latch on the door that works. There was a small rug in the bunk-room. Jack and I sprawled onto a table; we dozed for nearly half an hour.

We swung along easily to Cowles Cove Lodge. Doggone't 'twas nice going. Scarcely an hill and "nerry" a climb. We ate lunch at the lodge. It's a little bit of a thing and squats on a small

Montclair Glen Lodge, 1935.
GMC photograph collection.

cliff which overlooks a natural waterfall. The brook was full. The water rushed over the brink, swooped downward, flew into shimmering pieces when it struck the rocks below. Sun, streaming through the trees, made a rainbow of the lazy mist.

The trail from here to camp was hell. The day was the hottest we had had since we left. We hadn't minded that so much during the morning in the woods. There weren't any now. A forest fire had ruined them, much of the trail followed rock ridges. In addition to this, the trail refused to remain level for more than a hundred yards.

We reached the summit of Burnt Rock Mountain. It was well worth the climb to see the view of Le Lion Couchant from there. The peak alone was visible. It struck up majestically, rising above the notch which separates Ira and Ethan Allan [Allen] mountains. The rock cone and devil's cliff, we would be climbing them tomorrow!!!

I shall never forget climbing one of the side slopes of Ira Allan. A brook had merged with the trail. We slopped along. Sweat oozed from every pore and now and then would tantalize you by hanging on the end of your nose. Our feet were cool. About a half an hour of it was enough for the time being. We took off our packs and sat in the brook. Jack sillily dabbled water on himself in one pool and I in another. There was only one trouble, the pools weren't deep enough. Perhaps it was just as well as our clothes would have weighed far too much if we had submerged. Our pants were heavy enough as it was.

We reached camp about five o'clock. It seemed good to grin at each other, "set still and do nawthin'." We started supper after an hour. There was plenty to eat, with a real luxury for dessert—a pound comb of honey. As we fell asleep, porkys picknicked in the front yard. I asked Jack if he had brought in the clothes-line. A weak "uh-huh" and a yawn from his bunk.

JULY 29TH.

Left Montclair Glen 9:15 A.M.
Arr. Le Lion Couchant 11:00 A.M.
Left Le Lion Couchant 1:30 P.M.
Arr. Thompson's (Bolton) 4:30 P.M.
Trail – 7.5 mi.

As soon as I had dressed, I went outside to get wood. I had just gone through the gate when I noticed the clothes-line—or rather the remains of it. Jack had taken it from the trees but had not brought it inside the cabin. Porkies had taken care of it instead. They had fixed it!! I doubt it would have held a newspaper—shreds, shreds, fuzzy shreds, that's all there was left of it.

This day's hike held more adventures for us than any other day on trail thus far. There was the climb up Le Lion. Previous visits had made this mountain one of my favorites of all the Green Mountains. A short walk from camp brought us to the first sharp rise of the ascent. It took us over the "toe-nails" and onto the outstretched "legs" of the lion. Rocks—heaps of them, narrow ridges of them, stretches of them—formed the surface of the trail. Gnarled trees—sprawling, leaning, standing—grew on either side of the pathway.

Signpost in Bolton, 1930s.
GMC photograph collection.

Mrs. Thompson's house, Bolton, 1931.
GMC photograph collection.

As we proceeded, we could see impressive views of the summit of the mountain—a huge rock cone. It made you feel insignificantly small, it challenged you, it would chuckle at you when a piece of rock fell from the cliffs. At last, we reached the place where the cliffs tower almost directly over the trail. What a climb followed!!

The trail, for the first few rods, ascends directly and then veers to the left and to the west. As soon as we had climbed about a hundred feet, a gale of wind struck us. Fortunately it was from the west and tended to glue us to the rocks instead of sweeping us from them. Higher—slowly higher—still more slowly higher—the trees were far below us now. They looked like an unkempt lawn. The drive of the wind increased. It beat against us in torrents. Higher, still higher, the trail took us. A cement post ahead; a chipped and weather-beaten post ahead—at last! a chipped and crumbling post by our side. We had reached the summit!!!

Whish-sh-sh!! my hat decided to play [*sic*] a visit to heaven. A mighty blast of wind bore it aloft. It soared, it poised in mid-air, the gods were angry and dropped it—not to hell but down the side of a cliff. I was still angrier at the gods and told 'em so. It took me twenty minutes to perform the rescue.

After lunch, we rested a while and then started for the Winooski Valley—five miles away and nearly four thousand feet down. We had only been gone an hour when a terrific storm, which we had watched approaching from the northwest, arrived. Rain, driven by a mad wind, beat our faces. It cut them as if it had been hail. The rain did not descend; hurled by the gale, it swept across the narrow rock ledges. We staggered, swayed like a silly thing, shouted to each other but did not hear. We were soon unable to stand—I dropped on my hands and knees. A mighty gust of storm belched. Jack had not dropped. The gale picked him up as if he had been a twig and tossed him off the ledge. Luckily, there were some bushes about eight feet below. He landed in them like a bag of meal and crawled to where I was sitting in the shelter of a boulder. We crouched there for minutes; it seemed like an eternity. The storm rushed over our heads. When we began to get wetter, we knew that the wind had gone down—we moved on.

From this God-forsaken spot to the Winooski Valley, the trail was a wreck. Need I describe what we saw? Trees lay scattered about and huge branches of them occasionally fell from firm branches where they were hung. A chill followed the storm—it was bitter—and, as we walked, we could hear thunder in the distance and the thunder of nearby mountain streams.

———•••———

JULY 30TH. **Left Mrs. Thompson's 8:30 A.M.**
Trail – 11.3 mi.
Arr. Lake Mansfield Trout Club 1:40 P.M.

We went over the Bolton Mountain trail today. If you want to call it a trail, you may. If you want to call it a brook, you may. Jack asked if I had ever found it dry when I had been over it before. No—he believed me.

There is a rickety tower at the summit of the mountain but if you don't mind climbing one, go up it. The view is magnificent. Mansfield strikes upwards to the north. The sharp peak of Le Lion Couchant seems to pierce the sky to the south. Far to the East are the Presidentials—they are all visible on a clear day; Madison, John Quincy Adams, Samuel Adams, Jefferson, and Washington. Lake Champlain lies to the West, no longer a mere strip of silver, but a vast body of water, stretching for miles in either direction. It is inspiring to see it and beautiful to watch the shadows of clouds cross the Champlain Valley or climb the Adirondacks on the other side of the lake.

When we arrived at the Trout Club,[24] whom did we see but Professor Elliot B. White[25] of the English department at Dartmouth College. He was acting as manager of the house for the season. He invited us to spend the afternoon there and said that he would give us fine rooms, overlooking the lake, if we wished to stay for the night. We accepted his invitation.

I shall never forget the supper we ate. The dining room opened at six. Jack and I fairly fell through the door. A number of members slowly drifted in. Jack and I ate on. One by one, they finished and meandered out of the room. Jack and I ate on. All the guests had left. Jack and I ordered two helpings of dessert. The members eyed us as we clumped into the lobby, our hob-nailed shoes making little dents in the floor as we walked.

We visited for some time with the Whites. Half-past ten came. The lobby was full of people. Jack and I, with one voice, asked if we might have mid-night lunch. Commotion.

—————◦◦————

JULY 31ST.   **Left Trout Club 9:45 A.M.**

Trail – 6 mi.

Arr. Mt. Mansfield Hotel 1:15 P.M.

Our hike on the Long Trail today brought us to the climax of the trip inasmuch as we reached the summit of the highest of the Green Mountains—Mount Mansfield. It was a thrill to accomplish this as ever since starting, this peak had been almost as much of a goal as the Canadian border itself. We saw it first from Killington peak, a little blue bump on the horizon from there. It seemed awfully far away.

I am very fond of this mountain, even sentimentally so. To reach its massive shoulders and peaks thrills me. Little chills run up and down my spine as if they were having a picnic there. Reaching the Needle's Eye, a small cave-like passage at the southern end of the mountain, makes me feel like one who returns to his home after long absence and opens the front door.

After passing through the Needle's Eye, the trail ascends the forehead abruptly. It is a scramble which makes the cone of Le Lion Couchant seem practically level ground. There are two particularly steep places. Before some considerate people placed ladders up them, it was necessary either to use ropes or to sacrifice a good deal of finger nail.

After reaching the highest point of the forehead, the trail follows the profile of the mountain to a peak called the Nose. The hotel is located at the base of this cliff and to the north. When we reached the summit I looked down at the hotel. Mother was standing on the porch—waiting. It certainly seemed good to see her again. Although I have been away from home for over five years, I don't believe that I was ever so glad to see her as

Mount Mansfield Hotel, ca. 1925.
Courtesy of Vermont Historical Society.

I was at that time. Mother, Jack and I had lunch together. After a chat, we left her and went out to see how far we could descend into the Ice Caves.

We followed the rocky ridge of the mountain north for nearly a mile and then dropped eastward from the ridge to the mouth of the caves. It was a narrow passage about five feet across and twenty-five feet in height. We entered. About twenty feet from the entrance is a large boulder securely wedged. We fixed our rope around it and tossed the hundred foot coil down to the first level which is about twenty feet below and straight down. After lighting our head-lamps, we lowered ourselves, hand over hand. The temperature dropped as we descended and each time we breathed our breath streaked frostily in the beam. When we spoke, our voices echoed as if we were inside of a vault. We stood on the first level. Ice was beneath our feet; ice coated the walls of the cave. If you struck them sharply, sheets of ice cracked off and splintered as they struck.

We reached the northern end of the level and tossed the rope down to the second level. The coils slid down a steep and ice-covered plane. We slid down. It was much colder there. I looked for the hole which would let us through the ice floor and down to the third level. Owing to the cold winter, there was no break. I figured that the floor was about six feet thick. When I was in the cave before this, the preceding winter had been mild and the summer had been unusually hot and it was possible to drop to a fourth level.

Jack and I smoked a butt. The combination of the smoke and the frost from our breath made the cave so foggy that it was difficult to see. We clambered up and out. The sun felt hot and its light blinded us.

———◆———

Jack and I climbed the nose after supper to watch the sunset. It was beautiful. Colors tinted clumps of clouds and streaked overhead to light some eastern clouds. Lake Champlain was a perfect mirror—red changing to delicate pinks, pinks fading into blues, blues fading into greyness and greyness into darkness. The pines below, far below, murmured in the rising wind. We went down to the hotel and sat by an open fire.

Mother was playing bridge—contract bridge—Jack and I talked until we preferred to think.

AUGUST 1ST.   **Day at Mansfield.**

Jack's father and mother and my father arrived on Mansfield in the afternoon. As soon as they had put their cars away and changed into hiking clothes, we went out along the ridge, found a good place to sit down and had a talk fest until supper time. We continued it after supper. It seemed good to do nothing but visit and rest.

AUGUST 2ND.   **Day at Mansfield.**

I spent my time today travelling over the summit of Mansfield. It's the grandest place to wander about I know of. I've spent months there but each time I go out, I find new things to admire. In the morning, I walked over to the "Chin," the highest point of the mountain and about two miles from the hotel. In the afternoon, I walked southward and studied the cliff formations of the "Nose." I don't think that I have ever seen the White Mountains stand out so clearly as they did this day. They seemed just across the valley and beckoned to me to climb them. I left the summit of Mansfield on a previous visit, drove to them, and climbed Washington. I could see Mansfield from there and it called me back. I prefer Mansfield because the views are more intimate and long association with the mountain has made it seem like a home.

After supper the six of us climbed the "Nose" to watch the sunset. It was more lovely than the first night. There weren't so many clouds and the display of colors was much broader. We could see the flat Mount Royal to the north. It looked like a lump of pink sugar.

Shortly after sunset clouds engulfed the mountain. It was cold and the cables which lash the hotel to its foundation hummed in a northwest wind.

AUGUST 3RD.   **Left Mount Mansfield 3:50 P.M.**
                                                            Trail – 2.3 mi.
                                              Arr. Barne's [Barnes] Camp 5:10 P.M.

Mr. and Mrs. Eames left for home soon after breakfast. I was with my folks until they left, a little after ten o'clock. It made me feel a bit homesick to see them drive away but Jack shouted to me to come up on the "Nose" before we packed up. The scramble set me right again. It made me want to push on to the end of the trail—only about a week off now.

We packed after lunch—nearly sixty pounds apiece, for this was the last chance we would have to stock up until a day before the completion of the trail. We took the Hazelton Trail to Barne's Camp which is located in Smuggler's Notch, a deep cut on the eastern side of the mountain.

It seemed good to hit the trail again. We had started the last lap!!!

———•———

AUGUST 4TH.   **Left Barne's Camp 8:30 A.M.**
                                                            Trail – 6.6 mi.
                                              Arr. Whiteface Lodge 3:15 P.M.

When we started this morning, it seemed ages since we scrambled up Pine Cobble outside of Williamstown. The trail from Barne's Camp ascended the eastern wall of Smuggler's Notch steeply. We walked easily, beginning our day very differently than the first one when we walked briskly for the first few minutes and suffered for it. I might add here, whatever little lessons you learn on the trail, don't forget them. You may think that you are strong enough to do any feats after you've been out for a month, but you aren't. A fast, steep climb, directly following a meal is unwise.

As we reached the height of land, out of the notch, a striking view of Mansfield presented itself. The mighty sentinel, at the northern end of this particular range of the Green Mountains, seemed ever so different from the angle we looked at it. It seemed much higher and longer and the many scars on the eastern slopes stood out sharply—great gashes and timber slides.

From this point the trail runs in a northeasterly direction through slashed timber lands and, by easy grades, runs over to Sterling Pond, only a short distance from Sterling mountain which is near the northeastern end of the pond. Our hardest climb of the day was from the pond to the summit of Madonna Peak on Sterling mountain. The trail fairly leaps up ridge after ridge and then, in the last quarter of a mile, takes you up nearly four hundred feet to the peak.

We ate lunch at the summit and Jack took a nap after our scrumptious meal of raisins (they were always dry), dried apricots, and chocolate bars which were *whole*; we wagered that they wouldn't be that way after a few days out. No matter how carefully you pack them, they always look sick after a day or so in the pack. I remember once that a cooking spoon shoved clean through the bag in which we were carrying them.

While Jack was resting, I reconnoitered on the northern cliffs. I could see Whiteface Lodge; it seemed only a stone's throw across the saddle. It looked like a shell hole in the side of the mountain and the tin roof of the shack mirrored in the sunlight . . . . We reached camp about two hours later.

It has a magnificent location. There is exceptionally good water there—and that means something, for the water on the Long Trail is the one thing you miss more than anything else when you spend a night or so away from it. As you stand in front of the cabin and look at the saddle, two little blobs of rock stick up above it. They are the "Nose" and "Chin" of Mansfield. It was wierd [*sic*] to sit there that evening and be able to see a faint glow to the north of the nose—it was from the lights at the hotel . . . . We watched the glow increase with the darkness . . . . It was after nine, what a late hour to go to bed!!

AUGUST 5TH.

Left Whiteface Lodge 8:30 A.M.
Trail – 10 mi.
Arr. Ed Derby's Place 4:15 P.M.

Our hopes for a good night's rest were continually blasted during the late hours of the night as porkys chose our "front lawn" for a parade ground. I killed one of the group but the other members of the convention were too evasive. During the "wee sma' hours" we heard a crashing in the berry bushes which were only a few yards from the cabin. Judging from the noise of the foot steps and the grunting, we knew that a bear was having a little midnight lunch. We were glad that there were plenty of berries.

Today was our second real blisterer on trail. When we stopped for lunch at the Tillitson [Tillotson] farm in the Lamoille Valley, it was over 95 in the shade. We rested there for some time—we had green apples for dessert.

We pushed on and meandered upwards and northward to the summit of Prospect Rock; a beautiful spot overlooking the valley. But was it hot there!!!! There was a breeze drifting about but it was hot air and didn't help a bit. Jack's stomach had bothered him ever since lunch time, so we rested there for over half an hour. I was hotter when we left than when we reached there.

Hiker preparing to bury porcupine.
GMC photograph collection.

The last half mile to Ed's place was an easy one and it wasn't long before the usual farm dog greeted us with loud barks and wheelings of his tail.

Gee, but it seemed good to see the sun go down—not so good, as it was red, awfully so, and that meant another hot day for us . . . . I slept on the floor. A feather bed held no temptation for me, besides being hot, it would have been too soft.

———◆———

AUGUST 6TH.   **Left Ed Derby's 8:30 A.M.**
                                    Trail – 9.5 mi.
                                    Arr. Parker Camp 4:00 P.M.

Yesterday may have been a blisterer but the heat today surpassed all former attempts. We had had over ten hours of sleep so we were ready for anything that the trail might provide—we thought that we were but what followed took that silly notion out of our heads.

The first three miles weren't so bad, as the trail kept in the woods and the grades were easy, we reached Emery's farm in a little over an hour. From that point on, the heat began to tell. It was practically impossible to hike for more than ten minutes at a stretch. The Canadian Border seemed ages away, almost as far as it did when we were a hundred miles down-state. Each time that we flopped to the ground, the sweat streaming from our faces and making our eyes smart and everything taste salty, we wondered if we could possibly go on to camp. Thank God we had enough sense not to drink much water, that *would* have queered the act for fair.[26] We munched dried prunes to keep our mouths moist.

We reached the foot of Laraway mountain at 11:30 and rested for half an hour. We pushed on. Our feet weighed tons and we wished that it would rain hard, terrible hard! I don't think that the heat ever got me the way it did during the ensuing hour and a half. My heart beat like a trip-hammer. My breath came in aching gasps. Would it ever end, would it ever end, would we ever reach camp? Why wasn't there some water, fresh water? The water in our canteens was hot and tasted as if it had been burned . . . . A mountain stream roared in the distance!!! *We ran uphill to it!!!!*

The last quarter mile to the summit took us nearly beneath huge cliffs. Water slowly dripped from them. It was cool there. We reached the summit, had lunch, and went to sleep. It was after two when we awoke. From there to the camp, the trail was comparatively easy and we hit camp just before a snorting thunder storm. How cool it was that evening.

As we sat on the roof of the cabin, a long moaning of animals in the distance startled us. The sound grew louder. I grabbed my knife and laid it by my side. The moan changed to bellowing. It was awful. It sounded from the top of the ridge which is only a quarter of a mile from camp . . . . The next bellow was not so loud. The sound gradually diminished, although it continued for some time after we had gone to bed. Just what it was we do not know. Perhaps some cattle, pastured in an upland meadow, had broken loose during the storm and had lost their way in the mountains. Perhaps one of them was hurt . . . . We were scared, "plenteee." Believe me, a gat[27] would have made us feel much more comfortable. In fact, I would advise a person hiking the northern end of the trail to carry one. That end is much wilder than any of the rest and signs of bear and wild-cat are much more common than on the southern and central parts of the trail.

<hr/>

AUGUST 7TH.   **Left Parker Camp 7:40 A.M.**
                                                       Trail – 11.4 mi.
                                    Arr. Belvidere Fire Station 4:15 P.M.

After an early breakfast we hit up over Butternut mountain, on the way to the Fire Warden's cabin on the summit of Belvidere. From the triangulation station on the summit of Butternut, the trail descended steeply to the foot of Bowen mountain. An abandoned logging road made the going easy and we swung along rapidly. The day was cool an' everything was "hunky-dory."

Our good fortune ended at Bowen mountain. Although the trail from there to Ritterbush Camp, near Ritterbush Pond, was well marked, it was thickly grown over with nearly every kind of underbrush imaginable. The tall nettles were the worst. Each time you struck one, a thousand sharp prickers stung you. They made your face burn and your hands bleed from trying to push a few of them out of the way. It was impossible to see the ground and more than once we tripped over a "submerged" log and fell sprawling. We would swear, pick ourselves up and go on.

Ridges, ridges, ridges—would the trail ever stop following them. They seemed interminable. We finally reached the end of the last one and the trail, in Long Trail manner, fell for a hundred feet. I have often wondered why the trail-builders didn't let you down gradually. It would have caused us less wondering and the poor devils coming the other way would have a much easier climb. We reached Devil's Gulch, a thousand feet down and less than a mile from the end of the ridge.

We ate lunch at Ritterbush Camp, climbed steeply up the eastern walls of the gulch and arrived at the Eden highway. Belvidere was just across the road, massive and grand.

The trail up the mountain followed another old road for some distance before swinging up onto the first shoulder. The road runs through a narrow pass between Belvidere and Tillitson [Tillotson] peaks. From the place where the trail turned off, to the summit, was a hell of a climb.

Mr. Tatreau [Tatro][28] is the warden on Belvidere. He is a young man, about twenty-eight, in contrast to other wardens whom we met on the Long Trail and whom we have met at other times. We asked him how he happened to have that position. He replied, that just as we all have dreams of what we would like to be when we get out in the world, that job was his dream. He loves the mountains, is happy there, and every third week, has a chance to go down into the valley and see his wife, while another man takes charge.

We climbed the tower a short while after we reached the peak. The visibility was esceptionall [*sic*] fine. We looked at the views to the south, east, and west. We gazed at the view to the north. There were Jay Peaks—all three of them. There were the last peaks of the trail and, from the summit of the highest, the boundary was only eight miles away! If all went well, we would be over them the following day and have a beer or two in the evening.

About ten o'clock in the evening, the warden suggested a feed. We weren't particularly hungry but thought that a cup of coffee and some new biscuits would go pretty good. If we had limited ourselves to that, Jack and I wouldn't have wanted to stay on for days when we went to bed. As it was, we started off with vegetable soup—thick with plenty of crackers. This was followed by a huge green-apple shortcake. OH BOY, what a feed it was; not dainty but, gawd, how lackadazical we felt when we finished. We sat out in front of the cabin for nearly an hour after our lunch. The cool air seemed good; very good.

AUGUST 8TH.

Left Belvidere 10:30 A.M.
Trail – 6.6 mi.
Arr. Albert Deuso's 5:30 P.M.

On account of the "evening's festivities," we slept later than usual and even when we did get up, felt groggy and would have liked to have stayed on for a day or so. After breakfast we helped the warden clean up the station—Mrs. Tatreau was coming up the next day—and then headed northward.

The trail zig-zagged over Tillitson Peak and Haystack mountain and then dropped, in characteristic manner, to Hazen's Notch. Except for one or two views from the ridges of Haystack mountain, the hike was not interesting. It was just a case of plugging along lazily and struggling up the slopes with more difficulty than usual.

The saddle between the two peaks provided two miles of tough going.[29] Jack and I mentioned more than once about the poor condition of the northern end of the trail. Not only was there a great deal of undergrowth but, in addition, the blazes were fewer and what there were, were in poor condition. One of the chief purposes of the trail is to provide means for fire-fighters[30] to reach the forests more easily in case of fire—they would have a fine time packing apparatus over the miles from Smuggler's Notch!

We ate our lunch by the Montgomery–Lowell highway which runs through Hazen's Notch and then hitch-hiked into Montgomery Center to buy enough supplies to carry us over the last day on trail.

When we packed in the morning, I discovered that I had lost my birth certificate on the trail the previous day. That being the case, I meandered over to the Town Clerk's office to see if I could procure some sort of a statement to prove that I am an American citizen. Whom should I meet on the way but Mr. William J. Wright, an alumnus of Vermont Academy in the class of '93, a friend of Dad's and an acquaintance of mine. What a lucky break that was!! Through his help, I was able to get a statement from the town clerk, Mr. Gardyne.[31]

After doing our errands and giving the town the "oh-oh," Jack and I rode out to the Deuso farm with Mr. Wright. The Deusos are a French-Canadian family, crude folk but as kind hearted as they make 'em. In the evening, Albert took us up the road a little way to see a Mr. Duffee. He is a retired army man who has a hut on the slopes of Jay Peak and is well

View of Jay Peak.
Courtesy of Vermont Historical Society.

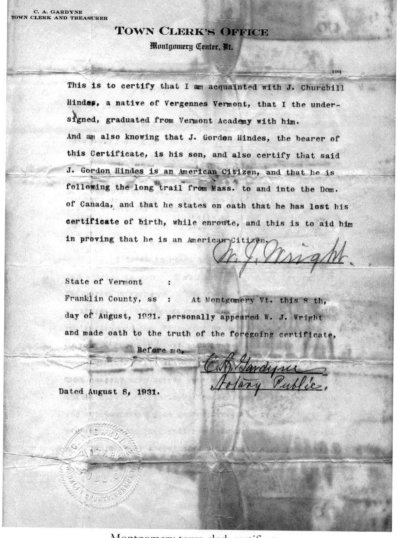

C. A. GARDYNE
TOWN CLERK AND TREASURER

TOWN CLERK'S OFFICE
Montgomery Center, Vt.

193

This is to certify that I am acquainted with J. Churchill
Hindes, a native of Vergennes Vermont, that I the under-
signed, graduated from Vermont Academy with him.
And am also knowing that J. Gordon Hindes, the bearer of
this Certificate, is his son, and also certify that said
J. Gordon Hindes is an American Citizen, and that he is
following the long trail from Mass. to and into the Dom.
of Canada, and that he states on oath that he has lost his
certificate of birth, while enroute, and this is to aid him
in proving that he is an American Citizen.

W. J. Wright.

State of Vermont :
Franklin County, ss : At Montgomery Vt. this 8 th,
day of August, 1931. personally appeared W. J. Wright
and made oath to the truth of the foregoing certificate,

Before me,

E. R. Gardyne
Notary Public,

Dated August 8, 1931.

Montgomery town clerk certificate.
Courtesy of Hindes family.

acquainted with the trail from that point to the border. After talking with
him for some time, we decided to go over to Highwater, Quebec, spend
Sunday night there and have Dad meet us at the United States' Custom's
House in North Troy on the following morning.

AUGUST 9TH.   **Day at the Deusos.**

Jack was taken sick with a touch of ptomaine poisoning during the night so it was impossible for us to push on. The kid surely has had more than his share of tough luck on the trail. What with his stomach upset, blistered feet, and a turned ankle, he deserves a lot of credit for sticking it out. It's a hard enough job for a well person to pack about forty-five pounds over two hundred and seventy-six miles of mountain trail.

I tried to reach Dad on the telephone that evening—tried is good! I cranked and cranked for central. There was no response. I waited a little while and cranked again. A voice came over the phone saying that central wouldn't be in the office until the next morning. I banged down the receiver and hunted up Madame Deuso to find out just what sort of a system it was. She explained that central only worked from 8:30 until noon and from one until four-thirty in the afternoon. I then asked if there was a telegraph office near there. She replied that the nearest one was in a rail-road station nearly twenty miles away and that by the time we could get there in the auto, the station master would have gone home and wouldn't budge for anyone—even in a case of life or death. While on the topic of telephones, telegraphs, and the like, I asked her how many parties there were on their line. She said, forty-two. I had heard of them running up as high as twenty-five and had used ones as high as twenty, but forty-two—no wonder news travels fast around Montgomery Center!!

—————•◆•—————

AUGUST 10TH.   **Day at the Deusos.**

Jack felt pretty weak this morning, so we decided to stay over another day. He got up for lunch but, after a short walk, went upstairs to take a nap.

While Jack was napping, Albert took me for a ride in the car. He said he didn't feel like "a-hayin' it." We drove over through Hazen's Notch. When we came back, whom should we see in Montgomery Center but Duffee. He had a thirty-thirty over his shoulder and a bottle in his pocket. His face fairly beamed and he walked unsteadily. Albert remarked that he would probably come up the road to his hut the next morning—if he had sobered up enough for that.

Jack had dressed when we got back to the farm and was out fooling around with the dog and Madame Deuso's grandson. He seemed much better but after he told me that he had had some more of the famous Deuso beer, I wasn't surprised. The Deusos had good beer. I had had some the day before and had topped off each meal with a schooner[32] of it that day.

U.S.–Canadian border, Line Post 592.
Courtesy of Hindes family.

After supper, Jack and I took a hike to some abandoned farms and didn't get back until after dark. It was time to go to bed. We packed, however, before turning in—optimistic? No, determined.

————◆————

AUGUST 11TH.   **Left Albert's 9:30 A.M.**
                                                          Trail – 16 mi.
                                         Arr. Highwater Inn 5:30 P.M.

I am sitting on the porch of the Highwater Inn. A pork steak dinner, plus some port wine, is camped in my stomach. When I finish writing up this last day, I'm going to drink my fill of ale with Jack. *This* is life!

A short while before we were ready to leave the Deusos, Duffee reeled up the road and stumbled into the kitchen. He was in a bad way. He hadn't been there but a few minutes before he challenged Albert to a rifle contest. We all went out onto the porch. Duffee raised the gun to his shoulder and aimed it in the general vicinity of a trail marker some hundred yards down the road. By the way he was swinging his rifle around, he would have come closer to hitting a tree on Jay Peak which was directly in back of him. Albert poked him. He fell sprawling and cried pitifully. Oh well, we might be doing the same thing before we went to bed.

Jack and I left soon after the demonstration and in a little over two hours reached the summit of Jay Peak. It is a rocky cone and sharply peaked; more than that, it is the last peak which the Long Trail crosses.

The trail from the peak to the border was terribly difficult. Even if it had been well cleared and blazed, it would have been one of the hardest stretches of all. We encountered everything which makes for bad going: bogs, steep grades, shale, soggy leaves, and long, long, miles, they seemed long, long miles because we were so anxious to reach the end, because they were uninteresting miles, running through dense forest lands. On, on, on—water was scarce. On, on, on—slowly, because Jack's stomach wasn't feeling quite up to par. A clearing ahead, a clearing ahead, a straight broad clearing about twenty yards across, *a white post in the middle of the clearing—it was the Canadian Boundary!!!!!* We sat on the boundary stone, stood on the boundary stone, played leap-frog over it, and munched a few raisins, apricots, and chocolate bars beside it.

After a long rest, we followed the boundary cut eastward, sometimes walking in American woods and sometimes in the Canadian. After two hours, we reached a road and turned north on it. It took us to Highwater, a little hamlet with one Inn and the Canadian Custom's House just across the street from it. We checked into Canada and the Inn—JACK EAMES AND DIN HINDES HAVE COMPLETED THE LONG TRAIL OF VERMONT.

Appendix

LONG TRAIL LODGINGS
*An Annotated List of Green Mountain Club and Other Lodgings
Mentioned by James Gordon Hindes*

Balch Place. In North Clarendon, one mile south of Governor Clement Shelter. Operated by Mrs. Edmund Balch. Lodgings and meals.

Barnes Camp (1910–11). At southern end of Smugglers' Notch, in Stowe. Two-story frame camp built by Stowe lumberman Willis M. Barnes for his winter loggers. Open to hikers in summer. "Meals and Lodging by Day or Week. American or European Plan. Hikers' Supplies. Lunches put up. Afternoon Tea. Sunday Dinners a Specialty. Parcel post packages and other mail may be forwarded to the Camp. Elizabeth B. Taylor, Manager" (advertisement in 1930 LT guidebook).

Battell Lodge (1926–28). North of Lincoln Gap. Open-front shelter of peeled logs, built by Middlebury College's Forestry Department. Bunks for twelve. Stove, simple cooking utensils. Fireplace by big rock in front. Good water ¼ mile to the south. Burned down in 1937. Replaced by Battell Shelter in 1938 and again in 1967.

Beane Farm. In Hanksville, Huntington, reached by logging road. Provided lodgings for hikers as early as 1917. Operated by Mrs. Frank Beane (d. 1966), a kind, helpful woman, for over four decades. Reasonable rates. "Full line of supplies for Long Trail Hikers. . . . Will care for hikers' mail and packages" (advertisement in 1930 LT guidebook).

Belvidere Fire Station. On Belvidere Mountain. Fire warden's cabin. Water. Good views.

Birch Glen Lodge (1930). Between Appalachian Gap and Camel's Hump. Semi-open camp, built by Frank Beane, set in yellow birch forest. Double-deck bunks for twelve. Stove, simple cooking utensils. Good permanent water to the south. Renovated in 1999.

Boyce Lodge (1926). North of Middlebury Gap. "Beautifully situated" open-front lodge built of unpeeled spruce logs. Bunks for fifteen. Stove and fireplace, simple cooking utensils. Good water. Side trail, south of lodge, to Bread Loaf Inn.

Bread Loaf Inn. In Ripton. Landowner and conservationist Joseph Battell (1839-1915) founded the inn in 1865, bequeathing it and surrounding property to Middlebury College. From 1920, the inn housed the college's Bread Loaf School of English, to which was added the Bread Loaf Writers' Conference in 1926. "Bread Loaf is a post-office, a convenient point to which hiking outfit may be shipped and mail received. As our guests are hiking enthusiasts, we always have food supplies of all kinds on hand. The canned foods are put up in sizes which are just right for the packs" (advertisement in 1930 LT guidebook). George E. Allen, hiking in 1930, reported that the inn was reluctant to put up hikers who looked scruffy after a few days out.

Buck Job Camp. *See* **Swezey Camp**.

Buffum Camp (1922). North of Vt. 103, in Wallingford. Open camp. Bunks for sixteen. Stove. Good brook water to the west.

Carmel Camp (1921). Between U.S. 4 and Brandon Gap. Rectangular, closed metal structure with piazza, set in meadow with raspberry bushes. Bunks for twelve. Stove, table, bench, and some utensils. Good spring water. Five minutes from LT. Chittenden village 1½ mile away by highway. Replaced in 1949.

Cooley Glen Lodge (1918–19). South of Lincoln Gap. Built by Professor Will Monroe and friends. Open-front shelter of peeled logs. Pole bunks. Stove, simple utensils, table. Spring water to the west. Mary Bach, hiking in 1930, called the lodge "nothing but a porky-ridden shanty, with a battered red tin roof. . . . Inside, the table was eaten almost completely away, so were the poles one sat on. . . . The little sheet iron stove had almost rusted away." Replaced by Cooley Glen Shelter in 1949.

Cowles Cove Lodge/Shelter (1920). North of Huntington Gap. Built by Professor Will Monroe and named for Judge Clarence P. Cowles. Bunks for five. Stove. Excellent water. Replaced in 1956.

Derby Farm. Near Prospect Rock, in Johnson, north of Lamoille River. Owned by Ed Derby. Lodging and food.

Deuso Farm. In Montgomery Center, south of Hazen's Notch, between Jay and Montgomery. Owned by Albert Deuso. "Excellent food and lodging." Mail.

Fay Fuller Camp (1930). North of Vt. 9. Stone structure, designed by Paul W. Thayer of Wallingford. Cost $850. Camp named for wife of donor Fritz von Briesen. Built by Bennington Section. Bunks for sixteen. Two inside fireplaces—one for cooking, one for heating. Water from stream to the west.

Glastenbury Camp (1929). On Glastenbury Mountain. "All-weather" steel camp built by John N. Leonard, A. J. Holden, and Dr. L. H. Ross of Bennington, Professor Carl. S. Hoar of Williams College, John B. Clark of Williamstown High School, and W. W. Holbrook, Glastenbury fire warden. Bunks for seven. Stove. Fine view. Excellent water.

Glen Ellen Lodge (1918–19). At Glen Ellen in Fayston. Built by Professor Will Monroe and friends. Open-front shelter of peeled logs. Pole bunks "full width, should have balsam bedding. Poles so springy that little is required." Stove, cooking utensils. Rock-walled garden with native plants in front. Permanent water. Hikers warned of creating fire "in spruce tops or in humus soil, which in dry weather is inflammable, smouldering underground for long distances." Replaced by second Glen Ellen Lodge, built by Long Trail Patrol, in 1933.

Griffith Camp (1920s). Abandoned lumber village, near Roaring Branch, with boardinghouse and school still standing. Open-front lodge. Bunks for twenty-four. Stove, fireplace. Replaced by Old Job Shelter, built by CCC, in 1935.

Grout Job Camp. Abandoned lumber camp on Arlington–Wardsboro Road, now Stratton–Arlington (Kelley Stand) Road.

Hooker Farm. In Brandon, 2 miles west of LT and north of Goshen Four Corners. Owned by J. S. Hooker. Lodging and food.

Killington Camp (1926–27). On Killington Peak. Stone lodge built by the Killington Section for $500. Bunks, stove, and fireplace. Caretaker. Food, blankets, and lodgings available "at moderate rates." Sometimes called Porky Lodge. (Not to be confused with the still standing stone-and-wood Cooper Lodge [1939], north of the summit, built by the State Forestry Department.) The first Killington Camp was a round, enclosed, sheet-metal hut with bunks and stove.

LaChance Tourist Camp. On Peru Turnpike, east of LT crossing of Vt. 11. Several small cottages operated by Oliver LaChance. Lodgings and meals at "reasonable rates."

Lake Mansfield Trout Club (private, organized 1899). On artificial Lake Mansfield in Nebraska Notch. Dam was built in 1900. The main lodge "a commodious and well appointed structure." Lodging and meals available, unless needed by Trout Club members. Telephone reservation recommended.

Lake Pleiad Lodge (1923). South of Middlebury Gap. Frame structure built by Lake Pleiad Section. Double-deck bunks for twelve. Stove, simple cooking utensils. Water to the south. Fishing license to be had at Bread Loaf Inn for a small fee. Mary Back, hiking in 1930, wrote that the lodge was visited by porcupines and that "you must choose between suffocation or porkies." The lodge replaced a shelter that had burned down in 1923.

Long Trail Lodge (1923). South of Sherburne Pass/U.S. 4, across the road from today's Inn at the Long Trail. GMC's rustic clubhouse, donated by club president Mortimer R. Proctor and his mother Mrs. Fletcher D. Proctor. Built of native materials. Common rooms and bed and bunk rooms featured unpeeled birch logs and boulders. Stone fireplaces, verandahs. The LT passed through the building. Also several small cabins. Immensely popular vacation destination, open to the public. Leased to Treadway Service Co. in 1933, sold in 1954. The lodge burned down in 1968.

Mad Tom Camp (1922?). Between Bromley Mountain and Styles Peak. Open-front camp. Bunks for twenty-four. Stove. Good water to the east. Reported in good repair in 1931 by Long Trail Patrol. Replaced by Mad Tom Notch Shelter in 1934 and by Mad Tom Shelter in 1962.

Montclair Glen Lodge (1917). South of Camel's Hump at junction of Forest City Trail and LT. Open-board camp built by Professor Will Monroe and crew. Named for Monroe's hometown in New Jersey. One of first structures to use chicken wire to keep out porcupines. Four double-deck pole bunks, each sleeping three people. Table, benches, shelving. Stove, simple cooking utensils. Tent platforms, flower garden. Good permanent water. Fine view of the Adirondacks. Lodge replaced in 1948 by second Montclair Glen Lodge, ¼ mile farther south.

Mount Mansfield Hotel. On Mount Mansfield. "The Mount Mansfield Hotel Company invites all trampers to make the Mount Mansfield Hotel their headquarters while visiting this section of the trail. You will receive a hearty welcome. 25 new rooms with hot and cold water. Bunk rooms for hikers at lower rates if wanted. Open from June 1st to October 1st on the Long Trail. Fine Auto Road to Summit. M. C. Lovejoy, Manager" (advertisement in 1930 LT guidebook). To get the best views, the GMC recommended a two-day stay.

The first lodging on Mount Mansfield was a platform tent (1856), followed by a small hotel and carriage road two years later. The toll road was completed ca. 1870 and improved for automobiles in 1922. The hotel was rebuilt and enlarged in 1923. It was razed in 1964.

Noyes Pond Lodge (1925). North of Sherburne Pass. Open-front shelter on bluff above Noyes Pond. Bunks for twenty. Stove, simple cooking utensils.

Parker Camp (1924). North of Johnson. In poor shape and repaired, according to 1930 LT guidebook. Replaced in 1932 by another Parker Camp.

Pico Camp (1925). East of Pico Peak. Open-front shelter of peeled balsam logs, steel roof. Cost $450+. Bunks for twenty-four. Stove and stone fireplace. Unfailing spring to the north provides "only shower bath" on LT. Replaced by new Pico Camp in 1959.

Ritterbush Lodge/Camp (1923). South of Vt. 118. Open-front lodge. Bunks for twenty-four. Stove. During the summer of 1931, it was repaired and creosoted by the Long Trail Patrol. Replaced by frame cabin in 1933.

Roskenney Place/Farm (name and spelling vary). In East Clarendon, 6 miles from Rutland. Operated by Mrs. W. C. Lane. Lodgings and meals.

Seth Warner Camp/Lodge (1929). North of Massachusetts line, near County Road. Donated by William H. Beardsley and family of Springfield. Named for Green Mountain Boy who was a Beardsley ancestor. Bunks for ten. Stove. Replaced in 1938 by Long Trail Patrol for Bennington Section.

Smith Farm. In Cuttingsville, Shrewsbury, 2 miles from East Clarendon depot. Owned by Frank Smith. Room and board.

Sucker Brook Lodge (1920–21). Between Brandon Gap and Middlebury Gap. Built by Lake Pleiad Section. Open-front peeled-log structure. Bunks for eighteen. Stove, fireplace, simple cooking utensils. Outdoor table between two trees. Good water in Sucker Brook. Mary Back, hiking in 1930, reported that porcupines had chewed some of the lodge logs "nearly in two."

Sunrise Camps. South of Brandon Gap. One open-front camp and one enclosed steel camp (1925), the latter funded by Redfield Proctor of the Proctor Section. Bunks for twenty. Stove, simple cooking utensils. Water from nearby brook.

Swezey Camp. Between Stratton Pond and Prospect Rock in Manchester, at Buck Job lumber camp. Bought and fitted up as open-front camp. Donated by Mr. Swezey of Manchester. Bunks. Stove. A 1930 hiker, George E. Allen, found Swezey to be leaking and called it "the poorest camp on the whole trail." Reported in good repair in 1931 by the Long Trail Patrol. Later burned down and replaced nearby by another camp, constructed of lumber from torn-down camp buildings.

Thendara Lodge (1929). South of Harmon Hill, Bennington. Built by New York Section with funds from its Thendara Camp in New Jersey. Bunks for ten. Stove. Destroyed by heavy snow. Replaced in 1958 by Deer View Shelter.

Thompson's. In Bolton, 500 feet north of the highway. Operated by Mrs. George H. Thompson. Room and board.

Wells Dickinson home. Near high point of Peru–Manchester Turnpike/Vt. 11, 1½ miles east of LT crossing. Lodgings and meals.

Whiteface Lodge (1922). On south slope of Whiteface Mountain, ½ mile from summit. Built by Fred W. Mould of Sterling Section. Open-front lodge with metal roof. Bunks for eight. Good, permanent water to the west. View of Madonna Peak and Mount Mansfield.. Reported in good shape in 1931 by the Long Trail Patrol. Replaced in 1958 by Whiteface Shelter.

Willis Ross Lodge/Camp (1929). At east end of Stratton Pond, among spruce trees. Open-frame structure built by Worcester Section, under leadership of George F. E. Storey and Louis L. Bigelow. Named for trail builder Willis Ross of Rutland. Bunks for twelve. Stove. Good view to the west. Spring water 30 feet to the north. Burned down in 1972.

Notes

1. 250-mile-long. Until the LT was completed in 1930, the trail ended at Jay Peak. The 1930 LT guidebook which Hindes used, gave the trail's length as 248.5 miles. The next edition of the guidebook, from 1932, gave the distance from Massachusetts to Canada as 258.6 miles. For many years the length of the LT was given as 265 miles. The most recent 2007 guidebook lists 272 miles; recent mileage revisions are due to relocations of the trail.

2. Davy [Davey] Tree Surgeons. The Davey Tree Expert Company (1909) of Kent, Ohio, was known for its scientific approach to tree surgery. In 1930 it sponsored the Davey Radio Hour, a popular music program, for twenty-six weeks (http://speccoll. library.edu.kent/reghist/davey/hist).

3. Berkshire Hotel. The hotel at 23 Sumner Street in North Adams, Massachusetts, advertised moderate rates and long-distance telephones in every room (*North Adams [Massachusetts] Directory, 1922*).

4. horn pout. A fish, also known as hornpout, horned pout, mud pout, or mud cat, but most commonly as brown bullhead (*Ameiurus nebulosus*) (http://en.wikipedia.org/ wiki/Brown_bullhead).

5. Bennington monument. The Bennington Battle Monument, a 306-foot obelisk, was completed in 1889 and dedicated in 1891 to commemorate the August 16, 1777, Battle of Bennington, in which American forces defeated the British (*Vermont Encyclopedia*). The 1930 LT guidebook called it "the highest battle monument in the world."

6. Paradise Café. Paradise Restaurant at 431 Main Street was owned by James J. Playotes, who came to Bennington from North Adams in 1922. He first opened an ice cream parlor, which he gradually turned into a full restaurant (Hadwen. *Rock Ribs of Bennington Town*).

7. Mr. Holbrook. W. W. Holbrook, fire warden on Glastenbury Mountain, was described by another hiker as "very courteous and more than accommodating." He fertilized his garden with the carcasses of porcupines he had killed (*Vermonter*, February 1931). The Glastenbury fire tower and ranger's cabin were built in 1927. The last ranger left in 1949 (Levin. *Ordinary Heroes*).

8. gurry. Fishing offal (*Webster's Eleventh Collegiate*).

9. observation tree. A wooden ladder nailed to a tree on Bromley Mountain gave hikers a panoramic view. Marshall (Marsh) J. Hapgood of Peru gave the wooded summit to the state for incorporation in the Green Mountain National Forest (*Guide Book of the Long Trail*, 1930 and 1932).

10. A heavy wind of the preceding winter . . . Later in the summer Professor Roy Buchanan and the Long Trail Patrol "cleared out the very bad windfalls near Stiles [*sic*] Peak that were so seriously criticised last year and this trail is now in fine shape" (*LTN*, August 1931).

11. fern-picker's cabin. Fern pickers supplied florists with long-lasting fern fronds. Fern picker was a listed occupation in the U.S. Census (http://www.bls.gov/ncs/ocs/ ocsm/comf-fix.htm).

12. Wess Taylor. Wesley Ordway Taylor, Dartmouth College, Class of 1931. From Lewiston, Maine, he settled in Portland where he worked for National Casket Company (*Dartmouth College. General Catalogue, 1769-1940*).

13. Ed Marceau. Joseph Edward Marceau, Dartmouth College, Class of 1934. He was from Rutland where he later opened a dental practice (*Dartmouth College. General Catalogue, 1769-1940*).

14. Le Lion Couchant. French heraldic term, meaning "resting lion," coined for Camel's Hump by Samuel de Champlain, first European to enter Lake Champlain in 1609. The mountain was also called Camel's Rump by early English settlers (*Vermont Encyclopedia*; Barnum. *Place Names*).

15. architect Thayer. Paul W. Thayer of Wallingford, architect of the Long Trail Lodge (1923), his first major Vermont commission, and Fay Fuller Camp (1930). Thayer designed numerous houses in the state (*LTN*, Fall 2005).

16. Camp Sangamon. A boys' summer camp in Pittsford, founded by Leone E. Smith (1892-1957) in 1922. The camp was based at a working farm, and campers spent at least half their time acquiring and using practical skills (*Sangamon: Camp with Pioneer Spirit*).

17. Mr. Erickson. Hindes remembered the name incorrectly as Erickson. He is referring to Eiler Larsen (1890-1975). (The original spelling of his Danish given name may have been Ejler.) Larsen wanted to be the first person to hike the entire Appalachian Trail. In November he arrived in Rutland from Maine, carrying a fifty-pound pack. He intended to remain in Vermont until March and then continue south (*LTN*, December 1930). The native Dane seems to have made an indelible impression on all he met, not just on Hindes. The *Vermonter* magazine devoted a whole article, entitled "Living the Song of the Open Road," to Larsen, writing that he helped blaze the LT in 1927 (*Vermonter*, April 1932). Larsen seems to be the same Eiler Larsen who for over forty years was known as the official greeter of Laguna Beach, California, where he is remembered with a life-size wooden statue (http://articles.latimes.com/2008/jan/06/local/me).

18. jerkin. A close-fitting, usually sleeveless, hip-length jacket (*Webster's Eleventh Collegiate*).

19. New Boston. One of four New Boston's in Vermont, this small community in Chittenden was once the last stop on the Rutland–Pittsfield mail stage route (Swift. *Vermont Place-Names*).

20. DuVal trails. Otherwise known as Du Val trails. Two blue-blazed side trails from Watters Farm in Brandon to the LT at Brandon Gap and Bloodroot Gap. Built by Guy Du Val of New York City, they featured "rustic bridges over the brooks and ornamental stiles over the fences" (*Guide Book of the Long Trail*, 1930).

21. abandoned marble quarries. The first marble was sawed in Brandon in the early 1800s; the last quarry closed in 1937 (*Brandon, Vermont: History of the Town*).

22. Camp Kewaydin. Camp Keewaydin. A boys' summer camp, founded in 1894, on Lake Dunmore, north of Brandon (*Vermont Encyclopedia*: "Summer camps").

23. blast furnaces of Port Henry. Port Henry, New York, on Lake Champlain was a shipping port for local iron ore. It had one of the country's earliest blast furnaces (1822) (http://en.wikipedia.org/wiki/ort_Henry_New_York).

24. Trout Club. Lake Mansfield Trout Club. Dartmouth College faculty members were members of the club. Professor Howard N. Kingsford, M.D., served as club president during 1924–50 (Craig. *"History of the Trout Club"*). See also Appendix.

25. Professor Elliot B. White (b. 1889). Elliott A. White was associate professor at Dartmouth College from 1923 (*Dartmouth College. General Catalogue, 1769-1940*).

26. queered the act for fair. Queered the effect for fair. A slang expression; the meaning here is unclear. Hindes may be saying that he and Eames were trying to conserve water until they reached the day's destination.

27. gat. A slang term, short for Gatling gun: handgun (*Webster's Eleventh Collegiate*).

28. Mr. Tatreau [Tatro]. Mr. Tatro, fire warden on Belvidere Mountain, "has been a great deal of assistance in that region and has saved the [Long Trail] patrol a good deal of work" (*LTN*, August 1931).

29. two miles of tough going. During the summer of 1931, the Long Trail Patrol "found conditions quite bad in the less used northern end . . . where damage had been done by an ice storm last winter. These spots have all been cleared up" (*LTN*, August 1931).

30. fire-fighters. In the early years of the Long Trail, it was thought that the hiking trail could also serve firefighters who needed to bring equipment up a mountain in case of forest fire. The idea was eventually abandoned as impractical (Curtis, Curtis, and Lieberman. *Green Mountain Adventure*).

31. Mr. Gardyne. Charles A. Gardyne (1862-1945) was town clerk from 1911 to 1940; he also served as town auditor, 1912–16, and town treasurer, 1920–40 (Renée J. Patterson. *Email*).

32. schooner. Larger-than-usual drinking glass (*Webster's Eleventh Collegiate*).

Bibliography

Allen, George E. "The Long, Long Trail." *Vermonter* magazine 36, no. 2 (February) 1931.

Back, Mary Cooper. *Mary's Way: A Memoir of the Life of Mary Cooper Back.* Compiled and narrated by Ruth Mary Lamb. Bolton Landing, N.Y.: Ruth Mary Lamb, 1999.

Barnum, Gardiner. *Place Names on Vermont's Long Trail: From Wampahoofus to Devil's Gulch.* Waterbury Center: Green Mountain Club, 2007.

Brandon, Vermont: A History of the Town, 1761-1961. Brandon: Town of Brandon, 1961.

Burt, Craig. ["History of the Lake Mansfield Trout Club."] 195?. Typescript at Vermont Historical Society Library, Barre.

Curtis, Jane, Will Curtis, and Frank Lieberman. *Green Mountain Adventure: Vermont's Long Trail.* Montpelier: Green Mountain Club, 1985.

Dartmouth College and Associated Schools: General Catalogue, 1769-1940. Hanover, N.H.: Dartmouth College, 1940.

Davies, Jean S., and others. *Pittsford's Second Century, 1872-1997.* West Kennebunkport, Me.: Phoenix Publishing for Pittsford Historical Society, 1998.

Guide Book of the Long Trail. 5th, 8th, and 9th eds. Rutland: Green Mountain Club, 1924, 1930, and 1932.

Hadwen, George E. *The Rock Ribs of Bennington Town.* Bennington: Hadwen Inc., 1977.

Hagerman, Robert L. *Mansfield: The Story of Vermont's Loftiest Mountain.* Essex Junction: Essex Publishing Company, 1971.

Hunter, Herbert C. "The Weather of 1931 in the United States." *Monthly Weather Review* 59, no. 12 (1931).

Levin, Ruth. *Ordinary Heroes: The Story of Shaftsbury, with a Chapter on the Vermont Ghost Town of Glastenbury.* Shaftsbury: Shaftsbury Historical Society, 1978.

Long Trail Guide: Hiking Vermont's High Ridge. 26th ed. Waterbury Center: Green Mountain Club, 2007.

Long Trail News (LTN). Issues for 1930–33. Rutland: Green Mountain Club.

Manning's Bennington, Shaftsbury and Arlington (Vermont) Directory . . . . Springfield, Mass.: H. A. Manning Company, 1945.

North Adams (Massachusetts) Directory, 1922. Schenectady, N.Y.: H. A. Manning Company, 1922.

O'Kane, Walter Collins. *Trails and Summits of the Green Mountains.* Boston: Houghton Mifflin Company, 1926.

Patterson, Renée J. "C. A. Gardyne," September 23, 2008, personal email to editor.

Sangamon: The Camp with the Pioneer Spirit. [Pittsford], n.d.

Sherman, Michael, Gene Sessions, and P. Jeffrey Potash. *Freedom and Unity: A History of Vermont.* Barre: Vermont Historical Society, 2004.

Swift, Esther. *Vermont Place-Names: Footprints of History.* Brattleboro: Stephen Greene Press, 1977.

Vermont Academy: A History of Survival and Success. Saxtons River: Vermont Academy, [1989].

Vermont Academy: Annual Catalogue, 1928-1929 Saxtons River: Vermont Academy, [1928].

Vermont Encyclopedia. Edited by John J. Duffy, Samuel B. Hand, and Ralph H. Orth. Hanover, N.H.: University Press of New England, 2003.

Vermonter magazine. Issues for 1930–32. White River Junction: Chas R. Cummings.

Waterman, Laura and Guy Waterman. *Forest and Crag: A History of Hiking, Trail Blazing, and Adventure in the Northeast Mountains.* Boston: Appalachian Mountain Club, 2003.

Woodward, Paul. *Long Trail Shelter History: A Work in Progress.* 1999. Typescript at the Green Mountain Club, Waterbury Center.

Index

Page numbers in *italics* refer to illustrations.